Number Sense

Teacher's Guide

Glenda Lappan
James T. Fey
William M. Fitzgerald
Susan N. Friel
Elizabeth Difanis Phillips

Glenview, Illinois
Needham, Massachusetts
Upper Saddle River, New Jersey

Connected Mathematics™ was developed at Michigan State University with financial support from the Michigan State University Office of the Provost, Computing and Technology, and the College of Natural Science.

This material is based upon work supported by the National Science Foundation under Grant No. MDR 9150217.

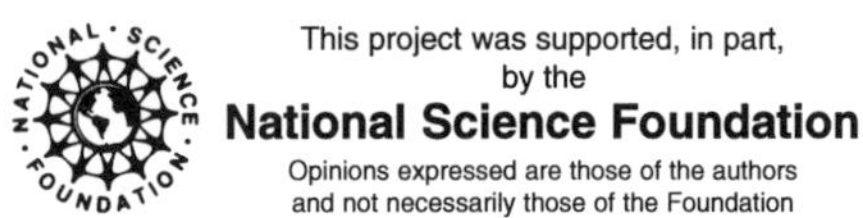

The Michigan State University authors and administration have agreed that all MSU royalties arising from this publication will be devoted to purposes supported by the Department of Mathematics and the MSU Mathematics Education Enrichment Fund.

Photo Acknowledgements: 5 © Nita Winter/The Image Works; 6 © I. Kostin/The Bettmann Archive; 7 (no roof) © Marc Pesetsky/Reuters/Bettmann; 7 (relief station) © Marc Pesetsky/Reuters/Bettmann; 9 © Ira Schwartz/Reuters/Bettmann; 12 © Stapleton/AP/Wide World Photos; 16 © Stapleton/AP/Wide World Photos; 26 © Roy Ellis/Photo Researchers, Inc.; 29 © Kelley McCall/AP/Wide World Photos; 32 © Photo Researchers, Inc.; 41 © Superstock, Inc.; 54 © Marty Heitner/Superstock, Inc.; 62 © R. M. Collins III/The Image Works; 67 © Paolo Koch/Rapho/Photo Researchers, Inc.; 68 © NASA

ISBN 0-13-180797-8
1 2 3 4 5 6 7 8 9 10   07 06 05 04 03

The Connected Mathematics Project Staff

Project Directors

James T. Fey
University of Maryland

William M. Fitzgerald
Michigan State University

Susan N. Friel
University of North Carolina at Chapel Hill

Glenda Lappan
Michigan State University

Elizabeth Difanis Phillips
Michigan State University

Project Manager

Kathy Burgis
Michigan State University

Technical Coordinator

Judith Martus Miller
Michigan State University

Collaborating Teachers/Writers

Mary K. Bouck
Portland, Michigan

Jacqueline Stewart
Okemos, Michigan

Curriculum Development Consultants

David Ben-Chaim
Weizmann Institute

Alex Friedlander
Weizmann Institute

Eleanor Geiger
University of Maryland

Jane Mitchell
University of North Carolina at Chapel Hill

Anthony D. Rickard
Alma College

Evaluation Team

Mark Hoover
Michigan State University

Diane V. Lambdin
Indiana University

Sandra K. Wilcox
Michigan State University

Judith S. Zawojewski
National-Louis University

Graduate Assistants

Scott J. Baldridge
Michigan State University

Angie S. Eshelman
Michigan State University

M. Faaiz Gierdien
Michigan State University

Jane M. Keiser
Indiana University

Angela S. Krebs
Michigan State University

James M. Larson
Michigan State University

Ronald Preston
Indiana University

Tat Ming Sze
Michigan State University

Sarah Theule-Lubienski
Michigan State University

Jeffrey J. Wanko
Michigan State University

Field Test Production Team

Katherine Oesterle
Michigan State University

Stacey L. Otto
University of North Carolina at Chapel Hill

Teacher/Assessment Team

Kathy Booth
Waverly, Michigan

Anita Clark
Marshall, Michigan

Julie Faulkner
Traverse City, Michigan

Theodore Gardella
Bloomfield Hills, Michigan

Yvonne Grant
Portland, Michigan

Linda R. Lobue
Vista, California

Suzanne McGrath
Chula Vista, California

Nancy McIntyre
Troy, Michigan

Mary Beth Schmitt
Traverse City, Michigan

Linda Walker
Tallahassee, Florida

Software Developer

Richard Burgis
East Lansing, Michigan

Development Center Directors

Nicholas Branca
San Diego State University

Dianne Briars
Pittsburgh Public Schools

Frances R. Curcio
New York University

Perry Lanier
Michigan State University

J. Michael Shaughnessy
Portland State University

Charles Vonder Embse
Central Michigan University

Field Test Coordinators

Michelle Bohan
Queens, New York

Melanie Branca
San Diego, California

Alecia Devantier
Shepherd, Michigan

Jenny Jorgensen
Flint, Michigan

Sandra Kralovec
Portland, Oregon

Sonia Marsalis
Flint, Michigan

William Schaeffer
Pittsburgh, Pennsylvania

Karma Vince
Toledo, Ohio

Virginia Wolf
Pittsburgh, Pennsylvania

Shirel Yaloz
Queens, New York

Student Assistants

Laura Hammond
David Roche
Courtney Stoner
Jovan Trpovski
Julie Valicenti
Michigan State University

Advisory Board

Joseph Adney
Michigan State University (Emeritus)

Charles Allan
Michigan Department of Education

Mary K. Bouck
Portland Public Schools
Portland, Michigan

C. Stuart Brewster
Palo Alto, California

Anita Clark
Marshall Public Schools
Marshall, Michigan

David Doherty
GMI Engineering and Management Institute
Flint, Michigan

Kay Gilliland
EQUALS
Berkeley, California

David Green
GMI Engineering and Management Institute
Flint, Michigan

Henry Heikkinen
University of Northern Colorado
Greeley, Colorado

Anita Johnston
Jackson Community College
Jackson, Michigan

Elizabeth M. Jones
Lansing School District
Lansing, Michigan

Jim Landwehr
AT&T Bell Laboratories
Murray Hill, New Jersey

Peter Lappan
Michigan State University

Steven Leinwand
Connecticut Department of Education

Nancy McIntyre
Troy Public Schools
Troy, Michigan

Valerie Mills
Ypsilanti Public Schools
Ypsilanti, Michigan

David S. Moore
Purdue University
West Lafayette, Indiana

Ralph Oliva
Texas Instruments
Dallas, Texas

Richard Phillips
Michigan State University

Jacob Plotkin
Michigan State University

Dawn Pysarchik
Michigan State University

Rheta N. Rubenstein
University of Windsor
Windsor, Ontario, Canada

Susan Jo Russell
TERC
Cambridge, Massachusetts

Marjorie Senechal
Smith College
Northampton, Massachusetts

Sharon Senk
Michigan State University

Jacqueline Stewart
Okemos School District
Okemos, Michigan

Uri Treisman
University of Texas
Austin, Texas

Irvin E. Vance
Michigan State University

Linda Walker
Tallahassee Public Schools
Tallahassee, Florida

Gail Weeks
Northville Public Schools
Northville, Michigan

Pilot Teachers

California

National City

Laura Chavez
National City Middle School

Ruth Ann Duncan
National City Middle School

Sonia Nolla
National City Middle School

San Diego

James Ciolli
Los Altos Elementary School

Chula Vista

Agatha Graney
Hilltop Middle School

Suzanne McGrath
Eastlake Elementary School

Toni Miller
Hilltop Middle School

Lakeside

Eva Hollister
Tierra del Sol Middle School

Vista

Linda LoBue
Washington Middle School

Illinois

Evanston

Marlene Robinson
Baker Demonstration School

Michigan

Bloomfield Hills

Roxanne Cleveland
Bloomfield Hills Middle School

Constance Kelly
Bloomfield Hills Middle School

Tim Loula
Bloomfield Hills Middle School

Audrey Marsalese
Bloomfield Hills Middle School

Kara Reid
Bloomfield Hills Middle School

Joann Schultz
Bloomfield Hills Middle School

Flint

Joshua Coty
Holmes Middle School

Brenda Duckett-Jones
Brownell Elementary School

Lisa Earl
Holmes Middle School

Anne Heidel
Holmes Middle School

Chad Meyers
Brownell Elementary School

Greg Mickelson
Holmes Middle School

Rebecca Ray
Holmes Middle School

Patricia Wagner
Holmes Middle School

Greg Williams
Gundry Elementary School

Lansing

Susan Bissonette
Waverly Middle School

Kathy Booth
Waverly East Intermediate School

Carole Campbell
Waverly East Intermediate School

Gary Gillespie
Waverly East Intermediate School

Denise Kehren
Waverly Middle School

Virginia Larson
Waverly East Intermediate School

Kelly Martin
Waverly Middle School

Laurie Metevier
Waverly East Intermediate School

Craig Paksi
Waverly East Intermediate School

Tony Pecoraro
Waverly Middle School

Helene Rewa
Waverly East Intermediate School

Arnold Stiefel
Waverly Middle School

Portland

Bill Carlton
Portland Middle School

Kathy Dole
Portland Middle School

Debby Flate
Portland Middle School

Yvonne Grant
Portland Middle School

Terry Keusch
Portland Middle School

John Manzini
Portland Middle School

Mary Parker
Portland Middle School

Scott Sandborn
Portland Middle School

Shepherd

Steve Brant
Shepherd Middle School

Marty Brock
Shepherd Middle School

Cathy Church
Shepherd Middle School

Ginny Crandall
Shepherd Middle School

Craig Ericksen
Shepherd Middle School

Natalie Hackney
Shepherd Middle School

Bill Hamilton
Shepherd Middle School

Julie Salisbury
Shepherd Middle School

Sturgis

Sandra Allen
Eastwood Elementary School

Margaret Baker
Eastwood Elementary School

Steven Baker
Eastwood Elementary School

Keith Barnes
Sturgis Middle School

Wilodean Beckwith
Eastwood Elementary School

Darcy Bird
Eastwood Elementary School

Bill Dickey
Sturgis Middle School

Ellen Eisele
Sturgis Middle School

James Hoelscher
Sturgis Middle School

Richard Nolan
Sturgis Middle School

J. Hunter Raiford
Sturgis Middle School

Cindy Sprowl
Eastwood Elementary School

Leslie Stewart
Eastwood Elementary School

Connie Sutton
Eastwood Elementary School

Traverse City

Maureen Bauer
Interlochen Elementary School

Ivanka Berskshire
East Junior High School

Sarah Boehm
Courtade Elementary School

Marilyn Conklin
Interlochen Elementary School

Nancy Crandall
Blair Elementary School

Fran Cullen
Courtade Elementary School

Eric Dreier
Old Mission Elementary School

Lisa Dzierwa
Cherry Knoll Elementary School

Ray Fouch
West Junior High School

Ed Hargis
Willow Hill Elementary School

Richard Henry
West Junior High School

Dessie Hughes
Cherry Knoll Elementary School

Ruthanne Kladder
Oak Park Elementary School

Bonnie Knapp
West Junior High School

Sue Laisure
Sabin Elementary School

Stan Malaski
Oak Park Elementary School

Jody Meyers
Sabin Elementary School

Marsha Myles
East Junior High School

Mary Beth O'Neil
Traverse Heights Elementary School

Jan Palkowski
East Junior High School

Karen Richardson
Old Mission Elementary School

Kristin Sak
Bertha Vos Elementary School

Mary Beth Schmitt
East Junior High School

Mike Schrotenboer
Norris Elementary School

Gail Smith
Willow Hill Elementary School

Karrie Tufts
Eastern Elementary School

Mike Wilson
East Junior High School

Tom Wilson
West Junior High School

Minnesota

Minneapolis

Betsy Ford
Northeast Middle School

New York

East Elmhurst

Allison Clark
Louis Armstrong Middle School

Dorothy Hershey
Louis Armstrong Middle School

J. Lewis McNeece
Louis Armstrong Middle School

Rossana Perez
Louis Armstrong Middle School

Merna Porter
Louis Armstrong Middle School

Marie Turini
Louis Armstrong Middle School

North Carolina

Durham

Everly Broadway
Durham Public Schools

Thomas Carson
Duke School for Children

Mary Hebrank
Duke School for Children

Bill O'Connor
Duke School for Children

Ruth Pershing
Duke School for Children

Peter Reichert
Duke School for Children

Elizabeth City

Rita Banks
Elizabeth City Middle School

Beth Chaundry
Elizabeth City Middle School

Amy Cuthbertson
Elizabeth City Middle School

Deni Dennison
Elizabeth City Middle School

Jean Gray
Elizabeth City Middle School

John McMenamin
Elizabeth City Middle School

Nicollette Nixon
Elizabeth City Middle School

Malinda Norfleet
Elizabeth City Middle School

Joyce O'Neal
Elizabeth City Middle School

Clevie Sawyer
Elizabeth City Middle School

Juanita Shannon
Elizabeth City Middle School

Terry Thorne
Elizabeth City Middle School

Rebecca Wardour
Elizabeth City Middle School

Leora Winslow
Elizabeth City Middle School

Franklinton

Susan Haywood
Franklinton Elementary School

Clyde Melton
Franklinton Elementary School

Louisburg

Lisa Anderson
Terrell Lane Middle School

Jackie Frazier
Terrell Lane Middle School

Pam Harris
Terrell Lane Middle School

Ohio

Toledo

Bonnie Bias
Hawkins Elementary School

Marsha Jackish
Hawkins Elementary School

Lee Jagodzinski
DeVeaux Junior High School

Norma J. King
Old Orchard Elementary School

Margaret McCready
Old Orchard Elementary School

Carmella Morton
DeVeaux Junior High School

Karen C. Rohrs
Hawkins Elementary School

Marie Sahloff
DeVeaux Junior High School

L. Michael Vince
McTigue Junior High School

Brenda D. Watkins
Old Orchard Elementary School

Oregon

Canby

Sandra Kralovec
Ackerman Middle School

Portland

Roberta Cohen
Catlin Gabel School

David Ellenberg
Catlin Gabel School

Sara Normington
Catlin Gabel School

Karen Scholte-Arce
Catlin Gabel School

West Linn

Marge Burack
Wood Middle School

Tracy Wygant
Athey Creek Middle School

Pennsylvania

Pittsburgh

Sheryl Adams
Reizenstein Middle School

Sue Barie
Frick International Studies Academy

Suzie Berry
Frick International Studies Academy

Richard Delgrosso
Frick International Studies Academy

Janet Falkowski
Frick International Studies Academy

Joanne George
Reizenstein Middle School

Harriet Hopper
Reizenstein Middle School

Chuck Jessen
Reizenstein Middle School

Ken Labuskes
Reizenstein Middle School

Barbara Lewis
Reizenstein Middle School

Sharon Mihalich
Reizenstein Middle School

Marianne O'Connor
Frick International Studies Academy

Mark Sammartino
Reizenstein Middle School

Washington

Seattle

Chris Johnson
University Preparatory Academy

Rick Purn
University Preparatory Academy

Contents

Overview

It's hard to imagine trying to describe and reason about the objects and events in our world without using numbers and arithmetic relations and operations at every turn. We use whole numbers, fractions, and decimals to describe length, area, volume, mass, time, and population; we use operations on those numbers to derive new insights from known information. The basic ability to reason about quantities is called *number sense.* Number sense is a complex set of skills and understandings encompassing the abilities to read and write numbers in various ways; to order numbers; to use numbers as measurements; to choose operations on numbers that will help to answer important questions; and to perform operations with appropriate methods, including estimating, making approximate calculations, and using calculating tools.

Middle grades students have been using numbers and arithmetic operations since they entered elementary school. However, flexible and powerful number sense develops over a long period of instruction and maturation. Furthermore, elementary school arithmetic seldom involves the large numbers and complex quantitative situations that are needed for describing and reasoning about many realistic and important situations.

In nearly every problem in this unit, students will deal with data that describe real-world conditions and issues, particularly environmental issues, and that data will often involve very large numbers. Investigation 1 sets the scene for the work students will encounter. Investigation 2 will help students to develop benchmarks for making sense of large numbers used in measurements. Investigations 3 and 4 will help them to make sense of numbers involving millions, billions, or trillions; to read and write large numbers using scientific notation; and to order large numbers. Investigations 5 and 6 will help them to develop several ways to compare large numbers.

The Mathematics in *Data Around Us*

Because *Data Around Us* is the closing unit in the grade 7 Connected Mathematics curriculum, it has objectives beyond developing the specific mathematical skills and understandings that comprise number sense. It offers students an opportunity to pull together many of the ideas and skills that they have been developing about proportional reasoning, area and volume, and algebra. The topic of number sense does not have the inexorable logical development that many areas of mathematics follow; the ideas may be presented in many ways. The conception of number sense that led to the sequence of topics used in this unit is as follows:

Reasoning about quantity begins with *awareness of magnitude,* or relative size. It involves the ability to work with both relative magnitude—including comparing and ordering numbers—and absolute magnitude—involving making sense of very large or very small numbers by building comparative analogies that are personally meaningful. An awareness of magnitude leads to a sense of *measurement,* the understanding that both units and counts are essential for describing quantity. The related idea that counts must be represented in an efficient way leads to an awareness of the various systems of *numeration.* Numerical information can be used to make decisions by *comparison* or to derive new information by performing *operations* on given data.

The six investigations in *Data Around Us* expose students to the ideas of number sense in roughly this order.

Mathematical and Problem-Solving Goals

D*ata Around Us* was created to help students

- Choose sensible units for measuring
- Build a repertoire of benchmarks to relate unfamiliar things to things that are personally meaningful
- Read, write, and interpret the large numbers that occur in real-life measurements using standard, scientific, and calculator notation
- Review the concept of place value as it relates to reading, writing, and using large numbers
- Review and extend the use of exponents
- Use estimates and rounded values for describing and comparing objects and events
- Assess the accuracy and reliability of numbers used to report information
- Choose sensible ways of comparing counts and measurements, including using differences, rates, and ratios
- Understand that a measurement has two components, a unit of measure and a count

The overall goal of the Connected Mathematics curriculum is to help students develop sound mathematical habits. Through their work in this and other data units, students learn important questions to ask themselves about any situation that can be represented and modeled mathematically, such as: *What is the role of measurement? How can benchmarks be developed to help make measurements readily accessible? Why is accuracy handled in different ways in different situations? When can special rate methods be employed in situations when ratios occur?*

Summary of Investigations

Investigation 1: Interpreting Disaster Reports

Accounts of recent disasters are used to challenge students to think about ways that numbers can be used to describe and compare important events. The work in this investigation gives the teacher an early diagnostic reading on students' ability to read and think about large numbers, to decide which numbers are accurate and which are estimates, and to hypothesize about how such numbers are determined.

Investigation 2: Measuring Oil Spills

Students read an account of the *Exxon Valdez* oil spill and are asked to think about the many ways that numbers are used to measure objects and events. They are reminded that a measurement consists of a unit and a count, and they review some units of measure in the customary and metric measurement systems. As part of developing a broad measurement sense, students begin to acquire a repertoire of personally meaningful *measurement benchmarks,* and they choose appropriate units for various magnitudes being measured. They develop two strategies for making sense of large numbers: finding other, more familiar objects of the same size; and selecting a smaller familiar object and determining how many copies of it would be needed to equal a larger object.

Investigation 3: Comparing Large Numbers

Through the exploration of data-rich problems, students review and further refine their technical skills in reading, writing, ordering, and interpreting large numbers. They continue to develop methods to compare large numbers. They are given opportunities to think about appropriate degrees of accuracy in the rounding of large numbers, and they are introduced to ways to estimate numbers and to interpret estimated numbers.

Investigation 4: How Many Is a Million?

Practical number sense encompasses the ability to deal with large numbers. To be able to reason about or interpret realistic information involving large numbers, quantities in millions, billions, and sometimes trillions must make some sense. In this investigation, students look at several common situations involving such numbers, and they are introduced to scientific and calculator notation for expressing large numbers.

Investigation 5: Every Litter Bit Hurts

The problems in this investigation focus on how individual instances of pollution and litter can lead to enormous environmental problems. Students work with data expressed as wholes and as rates, and they use rates or ratios to explore large numbers. In the process, they review some of the ideas they encountered in the *Comparing and Scaling* unit.

Investigation 6: On an Average Day

Students investigate a variety of intriguing data comparing the United States and Japan and are encouraged to consider what kinds of situations invite what kinds of comparison. They further develop their *operation sense,* the ability to choose an appropriate operation to combine two or more numbers to produce new information. In Investigation 5, students generalized from data for individuals to a larger group; here, they work with large data sets and compute rates per person or rates over a short time. They continue to explore the important issue of how two measurements can reasonably be compared, applying many of the ideas developed in previous units. By contrasting difference, multiple, and rate comparisons, students build upon and review ideas from the *Comparing and Scaling* unit.

Materials

For students

- Labsheets
- Graphing calculators
- Sets of base ten blocks (optional)
- Unit cubes (as many as you have available)
- Almanacs or U.S. maps
- Blank transparencies (optional; for sharing answers)
- Large sheets of paper (optional; for sharing answers)
- Stick-on notes
- Yardsticks (1 per group)
- Metersticks (1 per group)
- Bobby pins or paper clips (for making spinners; 1 per group)

For the teacher

- Transparencies and transparency markers (optional)
- Transparencies of Labsheets 3.1A and 4.2 (optional)
- Overhead graphing or scientific calculator (optional)
- Large U.S. map (optional)
- Almanacs or atlases
- Cardboard boxes approximately 1-ft square or with dimensions that represent combinations of 1-ft-square boxes, such as 1 ft by 2 ft by 1 ft (optional)
- Common objects to illustrate some units of measure, such as cup, pint, and quart containers; and foot rulers, yardsticks, and metersticks (optional)

Connections to Other Units

The ideas in *Data Around Us* build on and connect to several big ideas in other Connected Mathematics units.

Big Idea	Prior Work	Future Work
understanding and comparing large numbers	scaling quantities up or down; comparing quantities expressed in decimal, percent, or fraction form; comparing categorical and numerical data (*Data About Us; Bits and Pieces II; Comparing and Scaling; Filling and Wrapping*)	comparing growth rates and stages of exponential growth (*Growing, Growing, Growing*); making meaningful comparisons among data about populations (*Samples and Populations*)
choosing appropriate units of measure and understanding the notation used to express large numbers	choosing appropriate units for measuring distance, area, surface area, and volume (*Covering and Surrounding; Filling and Wrapping*); using exponents (*Prime Time*); selecting scales for graphs (*Variables and Patterns*)	analyzing data that describe attributes and behavior of large populations (*Samples and Populations*); using scientific notation (*Growing, Growing, Growing*)
estimating with large numbers	developing benchmarks for estimating with decimals, percents, and fractions (*Bits and Pieces I; Bits and Pieces II*); estimating populations based on population densities (*Comparing and Scaling; Filling and Wrapping*)	making inferences and predictions about large populations; developing strategies for estimating quantities based on analysis (*Samples and Populations; Clever Counting*)
calculating with large numbers	developing algorithms for performing calculations with fractions, decimals, and percents (*Bits and Pieces II*); applying ratios, proportions, and percent (*Comparing and Scaling*)	making predictions based on patterns of exponential growth or decay (*Growing, Growing, Growing*); making inferences and predictions about large populations (*Samples and Populations*); developing strategies for efficiently counting large numbers of objects or outcomes (*Clever Counting*)
determining population density	analyzing data about populations and groups (*Data About Us*); calculating and applying population densities (*Comparing and Scaling*)	using information about populations and exponential growth patterns to predict population doubling time and half life (*Growing, Growing, Growing*); using data about a sample of a population to draw informed conclusions and make inferences about the entire population (*Samples and Populations*)

Manipulatives

The investigations in this unit will be enhanced if you are able to obtain unit cubes and sets of base ten blocks—including unit cubes (ones), longs (tens), flats (hundreds), and blocks (thousands)—with which students can experiment. These are common items in elementary classrooms; you may be able to borrow these materials from your colleagues.

Pacing Chart

This pacing chart gives estimates of the class time required for each investigation and assessment piece. Shaded rows indicate opportunities for assessment.

Investigations and Assessments	Class Time
1 Interpreting Disaster Reports	2 days
2 Measuring Oil Spills	3 days
3 Comparing Large Numbers	3 days
Check-Up	$\frac{1}{2}$ day
4 How Many Is a Million?	3 days
5 Every Litter Bit Hurts	4 days
Quiz	$\frac{1}{2}$ day
6 On an Average Day	3 days
Self-Assessment	Take home
Unit Test	1 day

Data Around Us Vocabulary

The following words and concepts are used in *Data Around Us.* Concepts in the left column are those essential for student understanding of this and future units. The Descriptive Glossary gives descriptions of many of these terms.

Essential terms developed in this unit

customary system
metric system, international system of measurement, SI system
million, billion, trillion
scientific notation
standard notation

Terms developed in previous units

benchmark
compare
rank
unit of measure

Assessment Summary

Embedded Assessment

Opportunities for informal assessment of student progress are embedded throughout *Data Around Us* in the problems, the ACE questions, and the Mathematical Reflections. Suggestions for observing as students explore and discover mathematical ideas, for probing to guide their progress in developing concepts and skills, and for questioning to determine their level of understanding can be found in the Launch, Explore, and Summarize sections of all investigation problems. Some examples:

- Investigation 2, Problem 2.2 *Launch* (page 22b) suggests questions you can ask to help your students begin to think about appropriate units and benchmarks for particular kinds of measurements.
- Investigation 5, Problem 5.1 *Explore* (page 60b) suggests questions you can ask to help your students understand ideas about the growth of populations.
- Investigation 1, Problem 1.1 *Summarize* (page 11b) suggests extension questions you can ask to assess your students' knowledge about the derivation and use of large numbers in real-world contexts.

ACE Assignments

An ACE (Applications—Connections—Extensions) section appears at the end of each investigation. To help you assign ACE questions, a list of assignment choices is given in the margin next to the reduced student page for each problem. Each list indicates the ACE questions that students should be able to answer after they complete the problem.

Check-Up

One check-up, which may be given after Investigation 3, is provided for use as a quick quiz or warm-up activity. The check-up is designed for students to complete individually. You will find the check-up and its answer key in the Assessment Resources section.

Partner Quiz

One quiz, which may be given after Investigation 5, is provided with *Data Around Us.* The quiz is designed to be completed by pairs of students with the opportunity for revision based on teacher feedback. You will find the quiz and its answer key in the Assessment Resources section. As an alternative to the quiz provided, you can construct your own quiz by combining questions from the Question Bank, this quiz, and unassigned ACE questions.

Question Bank

A Question Bank provides questions you can use for homework, reviews, or quizzes. You will find the Question Bank and its answer key in the Assessment Resources section.

Notebook/Journal

Students should have notebooks to record and organize their work. Notebooks should include student journals and sections for vocabulary, homework, quizzes, and check-ups. In their journals, students can take notes, solve investigation problems, and record their ideas about Mathematical Reflections questions. Journals should be assessed for completeness rather than correctness; they should be seen as "safe" places where students can try out their thinking. A Notebook Checklist and a Self-Assessment are provided in the Assessment Resources section. The Notebook Checklist helps students organize their notebooks. The Self-Assessment guides students as they review their notebooks to determine which ideas they have mastered and which they still need to work on.

The Unit Test

The final assessment in *Data Around Us* is a unit test that focuses on using and making sense of large numbers.

Introducing Your Students to *Data Around Us*

Read through the introduction with the class, using these situations as an opportunity to begin to assess students' number-sense skills. You might ask questions such as these: "How do you read the number for how many people lost their homes in the hurricane?" "How do you read the number for the amount of people in the world?" "How do these two numbers compare? Which is greater? How much greater? How many times greater?"

Ask students to think about how some of these counts may have been determined: "How do you think the number of people left without homes was determined? The number of people in the world?" "How do you think it was found that $43 million worth of dollar bills would stretch 4100 miles? Do you think this is an exact figure or an estimate? Why?"

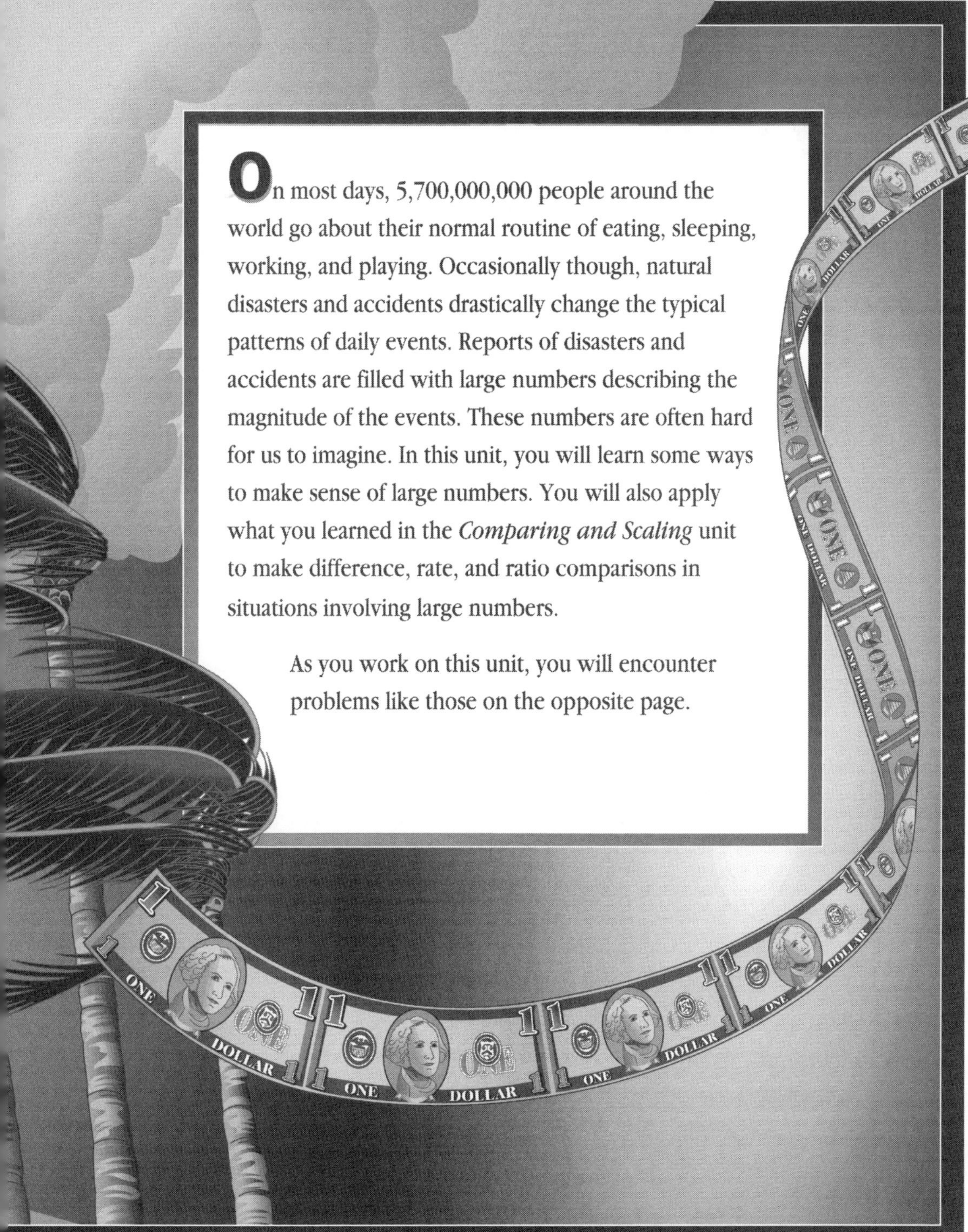

On most days, 5,700,000,000 people around the world go about their normal routine of eating, sleeping, working, and playing. Occasionally though, natural disasters and accidents drastically change the typical patterns of daily events. Reports of disasters and accidents are filled with large numbers describing the magnitude of the events. These numbers are often hard for us to imagine. In this unit, you will learn some ways to make sense of large numbers. You will also apply what you learned in the *Comparing and Scaling* unit to make difference, rate, and ratio comparisons in situations involving large numbers.

As you work on this unit, you will encounter problems like those on the opposite page.

This introduction is intended to interest students in what large numbers mean and how they are determined. It is not expected that students will resolve the questions raised in the discussion at this time.

Mathematical Highlights

The Mathematical Highlights page provides information for students and for parents and other family members. It gives students a preview of the activities and problems in *Data Around Us.* As they work through the unit, students can refer back to the Mathematical Highlights page to review what they have learned and to preview what is still to come. This page also tells students' families what mathematical ideas and activities will be covered as the class works through *Data Around Us.*

Mathematical Highlights

In *Data Around Us,* you will explore ways to reason with quantities in order to build number sense. This unit will help you to

- Choose sensible units for measuring;
- Understand that measurement has two components, a unit of measure and a count;
- Build a repertoire of benchmarks to relate the measures of unfamiliar objects or events to the measures of objects or events that are personally meaningful;
- Review the concept of place value as it relates to reading, writing, and using large numbers;
- Read, write, and interpret large numbers that occur in everyday measurements using standard, scientific, and calculator notation;
- Choose sensible ways of comparing counts and measurements, including using differences, rates, and ratios; and
- Use estimates and rounded numbers for describing and comparing quantities.

As you work on the problems in this unit, make it a habit to ask questions about situations that involve number sense: *What quantities or measures are used or needed? How can benchmarks help make my understanding of the measurements clearer? What is the degree of accuracy that I need to use in working with these measurements? If I am making a comparison, do I want to use a simple difference or would using a percent or a ratio be a better choice?*

The Investigations

The teaching materials for each investigation consist of three parts: an overview, student pages with teaching outlines, and detailed notes for teaching the investigation.

The overview of each investigation includes brief descriptions of the problems, the mathematical and problem-solving goals of the investigation, and a list of necessary materials.

Essential information for teaching the investigation is provided in the margins around the student pages. The "At a Glance" overviews are brief outlines of the Launch, Explore, and Summarize phases of each problem for reference as you work with the class. To help you assign homework, a list of "Assignment Choices" is provided next to each problem. Where space permits, answers to problems, follow-ups, ACE questions, and Mathematical Reflections appear next to the appropriate student pages.

The Teaching the Investigation section follows the student pages and is the heart of the Connected Mathematics curriculum. This section describes in detail the Launch, Explore, and Summarize phases for each problem. It includes all the information needed for teaching, along with suggestions for what you might say at key points in the teaching. Use this section to prepare lessons and as a guide for teaching the investigations.

Assessment Resources

The Assessment Resources section contains blackline masters and answer keys for the check-up, the quiz, the Question Bank, and the Unit Test. Blackline masters for the Notebook Checklist and the Self-Assessment are given. These instruments support student self-evaluation, an important aspect of assessment in the Connected Mathematics curriculum. A discussion of how one teacher assessed students' work on the Unit Test is included, along with sample pages of students' work.

Blackline Masters

The Blackline Masters section includes masters for all labsheets and transparencies.

Additional Practice

Practice pages for each investigation offer additional problems for students who need more practice with the basic concepts developed in the investigations as well as some continual review of earlier concepts.

Descriptive Glossary

The Descriptive Glossary provides descriptions and examples of the key concepts in *Data Around Us.* These descriptions are not intended to be formal definitions, but are meant to give you an idea of how students might make sense of these important concepts.

INVESTIGATION 1

Interpreting Disaster Reports

This investigation, in which students consider large numbers in real-world contexts, sets the scene for the work that students will encounter in this unit.

In Problem 1.1, Comparing Disasters, students read accounts of several famous disasters. They are asked to think about which numbers in the accounts are accurate and which are estimates and about how they might compare the disasters. In Problem 1.2, Aiding Hurricane Victims, students are asked to solve problems related to one of the disasters. For example, they are asked to estimate how much space and how many tents were needed to house the people left without homes after Hurricane Andrew hit south Florida.

Mathematical and Problem-Solving Goals

- *To consider some of the issues related to working with large numbers, including accuracy of reported numbers, methods of determining reported measures, and language used to make numerical comparisons*
- *To review operations with large numbers*

Materials

Problem	For students	For the teacher
All	Graphing calculators	Transparencies 1.1A to 1.2B (optional), overhead graphing calculator (optional)
1.2	Yardsticks (1 or more), blank transparencies (optional; for sharing answers)	

Student Pages 5–11 Teaching the Investigation 11a–11e

INVESTIGATION 1

Interpreting Disaster Reports

When a natural disaster or major accident occurs, news reports are filled with numbers describing the magnitude of the event. In this investigation, you will learn some ways of making sense of such numbers.

1.1 Comparing Disasters

To make sense of the numbers in a disaster report, you may want to ask yourself two questions:

How accurate are the data in this report?

How do the data from this disaster compare with data from other disasters or with things I am familiar with?

Read the following reports, which describe four well-known disasters.

On October 17, 1989, as baseball's World Series was starting in San Francisco, a tremendous earthquake struck the Bay Area, leaving 67 people dead, 3000 people injured, and $10,000,000,000 in property damage. As a result of the earthquake, many major roads and bridges were closed for weeks, paralyzing traffic.

In the early morning of August 24, 1992, Hurricane Andrew roared across the state of Florida from Miami to the Gulf of Mexico. With a top wind speed of 164 miles per hour, it destroyed thousands of homes and businesses, caused $20 billion in property damage, and left 15 people dead and 250,000 homeless before it moved on to Louisiana.

1.1 Comparing Disasters

At a Glance

Grouping: groups of 2 or 3

Launch

- Discuss the four disasters, and have students locate the site of each on Transparency 1.1A. *(optional)*

Explore

- Suggest that groups use a table to organize the answers to part A.
- Help groups reflect on the comparison methods they are using.

Summarize

- Have groups share their answers, and allow them to present their comparisons in a simulated news broadcast. *(optional)*
- Talk about the follow-up.
- Ask questions to assess students' grasp of large numbers.

Assignment Choices

ACE questions 1–6

On June 9, 1991, the top of 4795-foot Mount Pinatubo in the Philippine Islands exploded in a volcanic eruption that sent clouds of steam and ash into the atmosphere as high as 80,000 feet. The eruption poured lava as hot as 2000°F down the sides of the mountain. Pinatubo's volcanic ash fell to earth in a 60-mile radius around the mountain. The eruption caused the deaths of 700 people and destroyed 100,000 homes and a U.S. air base.

On April 29, 1986, equipment in several Scandinavian countries detected dangerous levels of radioactivity in the air. The radiation was from a nuclear power plant accident near Chernobyl in the Ukraine. The accident killed at least 34 people, contaminated land for miles around, and left millions of people deeply concerned about their health.

Problem 1.1

Use the information from the reports above to answer parts A–C.

A. Which numbers in the reports are probably very accurate, and which are probably only rough estimates?

B. Imagine that you are a journalist writing a story about these four disasters. Write several statements you could use to compare the disasters. For example, you might write, "The 67 deaths caused by the San Francisco Bay Area earthquake of 1989 were more than four times the number of deaths caused by Hurricane Andrew in Florida in 1992."

C. Describe the ways you found to compare the disasters.

Problem 1.1 Follow-Up

How do you think scientists, government officials, and journalists arrive at the numbers in their disaster reports?

Answers to Problem 1.1

A. See the Summarize section for a possible answer; accept any reasonable answers.

B. Possible answer: "The damage estimate from Hurricane Andrew was $10 billion more than, or twice, that from the World Series earthquake." "The Mount Pinatubo eruption caused more than ten times the number of deaths that the World Series earthquake caused." (Note: To be compared, numbers must have the same units. Measurements are commonly and most informatively compared by using differences—subtraction—or multiples—usually as a result of division.)

C. See page 11d.

Aiding Hurricane Victims

When a natural disaster or tragic accident occurs, people from around the world react quickly, sending clothing, food, medicine, and money. Many people offer their own time and effort to help the injured and homeless and to repair the damage.

When Hurricane Andrew struck south Florida, over 250,000 people were left homeless and without food or water. Relief poured into Florida from all over the United States. Making sure that food and supplies arrived where they were needed was a serious logistical problem.

Think about this!

Suppose you were in charge of a relief effort to help 250,000 people who lost their homes in a hurricane. How would you calculate the number of tents, the amount of food, and the amount of water needed for these people each day?

Aiding Hurricane Victims

At a Glance

Grouping: groups of 2 or 4

Launch

- Discuss the "Think about this!" question posed in the student edition.
- Have groups of two or four work on the problem and follow-up.

Explore

- Students need to measure the area of the classroom for question A and estimate the area of the school for question B.
- Distribute blank transparencies, and assign each group to a part of the problem for sharing in the summary. *(optional)*

Summarize

- Review the answers to each part of the problem.
- Talk about the follow-up question.

Answer to Problem 1.1 Follow-Up

Students will probably have many ideas about how scientists and journalists arrive at their figures. Help them to reason about why only estimates can be arrived at for certain counts while exact numbers can be found for others.

Assignment Choices

ACE questions 7–9 and unassigned choices from earlier problems (9 requires an almanac)

Problem 1.2

The United States Marine Corps and the American Red Cross sent relief supplies for families left homeless by the hurricane.

A. The U.S. Marines offered tents. Suppose each tent held 18 sleeping cots and covered 500 square feet of ground. Answer parts 1–4, and tell what assumptions you make to answer each question.

1. How many tents would have been needed to take care of all the homeless?
2. How much ground area would have been needed for all these tents?
3. How does the area of one tent compare with the area of your classroom?
4. How many people do you think could sleep in your classroom if a disaster struck your town? How many people do you think could sleep in your school?

B. The Red Cross provided cots, blankets, food, and water for the tent city and other shelters. They set up 126 feeding stations and 230 shelters. Answer parts 1–4, and tell what assumptions you make to answer each question.

1. If each person received at least one meal a day, about how many meals did each feeding station have to provide each day?
2. About how many students are served in your school's cafeteria each day?
3. How many cafeterias like your school's would be needed to serve 250,000 people?
4. The shelters housed a total of 85,154 people. What was the average number of people per shelter?

Problem 1.2 Follow-Up

The Red Cross reported serving 4,779,161 meals during the relief effort in Florida. How do you think this number was determined?

Answers to Problem 1.2

A. 1. $250{,}000 \div 18 \approx 13{,}900$ tents

2. $13{,}900 \times 500 \approx 7{,}000{,}000$ square feet (or more, to allow for space between tents)
3. The area of the typical classroom is greater than the area of one tent.
4. Estimates will vary.

B. See page 11d.

Answer to Problem 1.2 Follow-Up

Answers will vary. For example, the Red Cross may have had each feeding station keep track of the number of people served; or they may have estimated this number based on the number of people in the shelters and the number of days they provided meals for them.

Applications • Connections • Extensions

As you work on these ACE questions, use your calculator whenever you need it.

Applications

In 1–5, use the information from these reports of well-known American disasters.

The Blizzard of 1888 From March 11 through March 14 of 1888, a huge blizzard covered the eastern United States with as much as 5 feet of snow. The storm caused 400 deaths and $20 million in damage.

The Tropical Storm of 1972 In June of 1972, Tropical Storm Agnes moved up the East Coast of the United States, causing flash floods that killed 129 people, left 115,000 people homeless, and caused $3.5 billion of damage.

The Floods of 1993 From June through August of 1993, heavy rains in the midwestern United States led to flooding that caused 50 deaths, left 70,000 people homeless, and damaged $12 billion worth of crops and buildings.

1. Which numbers in these reports are probably very accurate, and which are probably only rough estimates?
2. Which disaster caused the greatest financial loss? How did you decide?
3. Compare the loss of life from the Blizzard of 1888 with the loss of life from Tropical Storm Agnes.
4. Compare the loss of life from Tropical Storm Agnes with the loss of life from the Midwest floods of 1993.
5. Compare the loss of life from the Blizzard of 1888 with the loss of life from the Midwest floods of 1993.

Answers

Applications

1. The dates, numbers of deaths (except for the blizzard), and the snow depth are probably accurate; the dollars of damage and the numbers of homeless are probably rough estimates.

2. The floods of 1993, because $12 billion is greater than $3.5 billion or $20 million. (This compares dollar values from quite different years, so inflation should be considered; however, the differences between the dollar amounts are great, so the floods of 1993 probably caused the greatest financial loss.)

3. Students may use either differences or ratios to compare these data. The blizzard caused 271 more deaths than did the tropical storm. The ratio of deaths from the blizzard to deaths from the storm is 400 to 129, or about 3 to 1, or about three times as many deaths.

4. The tropical storm caused 79 more deaths than did the floods. The ratio of deaths from the storm to deaths from the floods is 129 to 50, or about 2.5 times as many deaths.

5. The blizzard caused 350 more deaths than did the floods. The ratio of deaths from the blizzard to deaths from the floods is 400 to 50, or 8 to 1, or 8 times as many deaths.

Connections

6. Some possibilities: 10 ft by 50 ft, 20 ft by 25 ft, 4 ft by 125 ft, 12.5 ft by 40 ft, 16.7 ft by about 30 ft

7a. The estimate of the number of trees burned might have been based on estimates of the area burned, in acres, and the number of trees per acre. (Note: You may want to mention that this fire occurred on the same date as the famous Chicago fire and was actually more damaging. Also, at the time of the fire, Peshtigo's main industry was logging.)

7b. This problem is similar to the crowd estimation problems in *Comparing and Scaling.*

Extensions

8a. It is not possible to exactly fill a tent with 3-foot-by-6-foot cots. If the cots are placed right next to each other, 24 cots will fit in the tent. See diagrams below right.

8b. Possible answer: If the tent is filled with 24 cots, people will not have space to walk. If 1 foot of space is left on each side of each cot for access (giving 2 feet of space between cots), each cot would require a space of 8 feet by 5 feet. With these constraints, 12 cots can fit in a tent. See diagram below right.

9. See page 11e.

Connections

6. If the floor of a Marine hurricane-relief tent is a rectangle with an area of 500 square feet, what might the dimensions of the tent be?

7. On October 8, 1871, a wildfire destroyed the town of Peshtigo, Wisconsin, and much of the surrounding forest. More than 1200 people were killed, and 2 billion trees were burned.

- **a.** What method might have been used to estimate the number of trees burned?
- **b.** What similar estimation problems have you encountered in other Connected Mathematics units?

Extensions

8. Below are scale drawings of a cot and the floor of a Marine tent.

- **a.** How many cots could fit in a tent?
- **b.** If you were in charge of setting up the cots, how many cots would you put in each tent? How would you arrange the cots? Draw a diagram to illustrate your answer.

9. Read about great disasters in a world almanac.

- **a.** Which disaster do you believe was the worst of all time? Explain your choice.
- **b.** Make up a math problem about the disaster you chose for part a.

8a.

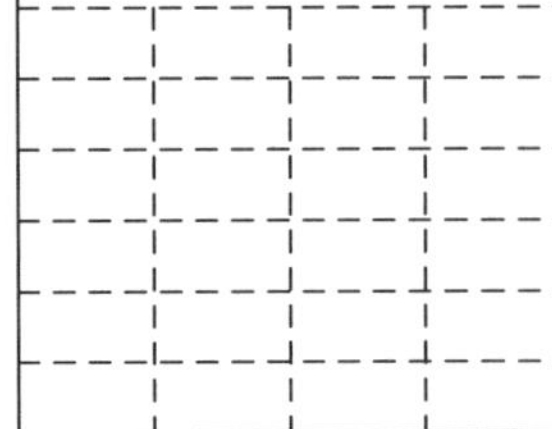

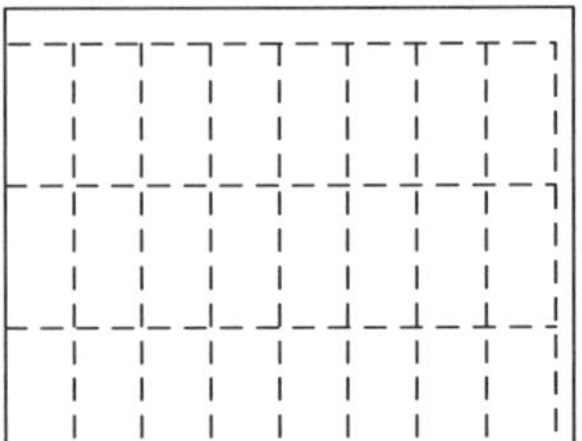

8b.

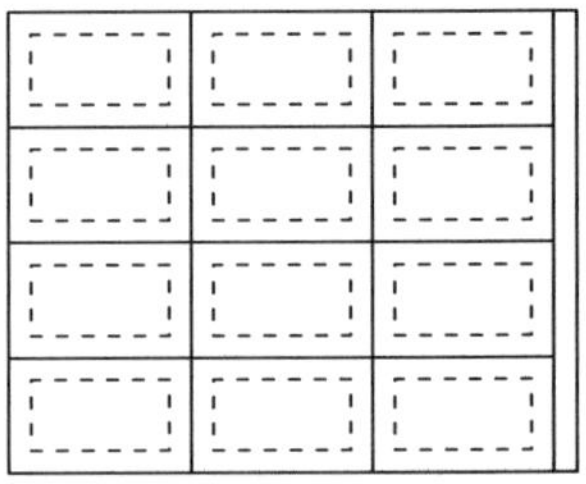

Mathematical Reflections

In this investigation, you looked at reports of natural disasters and accidents. You thought about how accurate the numbers in these reports might be and considered how the numbers might have been obtained. You also looked for ways to compare one disaster with another. These questions will help you summarize what you have learned:

1. What clues can help you decide whether a number is accurate or only a rough estimate?
2. In what ways can you compare data describing damage for one disaster with data describing damage for another disaster?

Think about your answers to these questions, discuss your ideas with other students and your teacher, and then write a summary of your findings in your journal.

Possible Answers

1. Extremely large numbers like 2 million, numbers with zeros in several of the lower place-value positions, and numbers for which it is hard to imagine an exact counting process are clues that may indicate a number is an estimate. Numbers that represent counts in which it is reasonable to expect that every instance was counted, measurements that don't contain several zeros in the lower place-value positions, and numbers that were probably derived from operations on exact numbers with no rounding may indicate more accurate numbers.

2. Data from two or more disasters can be compared by examining counts for similar units and using subtraction to find a difference or using division to find a rate or ratio. (**Teaching Tip:** If students don't come up with these ideas, you don't need to work on these ideas in more depth at this time. In Investigation 6, they will have an opportunity to consider these ideas more carefully.)

Tips for the Linguistically Diverse Classroom

Diagram Code The Diagram Code technique is described in detail in *Getting to Know Connected Mathematics*. Students use a minimal number of words and drawings, diagrams, or symbols to respond to questions that require writing. Example: Question 1—A student might answer this question by writing two headings, *Rough Estimate* and *Accurate*, and entering *24,000,000* and *4000* under *Rough Estimate* and *24,378,299* and *4235* under *Accurate*. The student would then underline the lower place values in each number.

1.1 • Comparing Disasters

This investigation is designed to provide you with information about students' facility in working with large numbers. The questions are framed to give students practice in expressing their ideas both verbally and in writing.

Launch

Focus the class's attention on the four disasters described in the student edition. If possible, display Transparency 1.1A, which contains a world map labeled with the location of each disaster. Help students to identify the site of each disaster.

Do you know of any recent disasters? Where did they occur?

For the Teacher: Bringing the World into the Classroom

You might ask students to pay attention to news broadcasts on television or radio over the next few days or to look through newspapers and news magazines for reports of other disasters, such as hurricanes, earthquakes, floods, and fires. They might bring in articles or information about these disasters and add their locations to the map.

Have students work in groups of two or three to explore the problem and follow-up.

Explore

Students will find different ways to organize the information in the disaster accounts. For students who are struggling, you might suggest they record their ideas for part A in a simple chart with these headings:

Probably quite accurate	Probably a rough estimate

As groups make progress on the problem, help them to reflect on the various means of comparison that they are using. Part C asks them to briefly describe these comparison methods.

Summarize

You might want to collect groups' answers to part A in a table like the following.

Probably quite accurate	Probably a rough estimate
67 people dead	3000 people injured
164 miles per hour	$10,000,000,000 in damage
15 people dead	$20 billion in damage
4795-foot mountain	250,000 homeless
700 deaths	80,000 feet of ash and steam
34 people killed	2000°F lava
	60-mile radius
	100,000 homes destroyed
	contamination for miles
	millions of people concerned

As groups share their statements for part B, help students to notice that the statements all compare numbers that have the same unit of measure (dollars, deaths, and so on) and that each comparison is the difference or the multiplicative relationship between the two counts.

If time permits, let students present their ideas about how to compare the disasters in a simulated television news broadcast; if you have the equipment, you might even videotape the reporters in action. Students' statements can also be written on large sheets of paper and posted as part of a display that includes news articles that students bring to class about other disasters.

The follow-up question asks students to compare how people in different professions might arrive at the numbers they report. Students will probably have many ideas about how scientists and journalists arrive at their figures—from NASA satellite monitoring of the atmosphere, weather-service monitoring of wind speed, and insurance-industry reports of damage, to official death reports. Help students reason about why only estimates can be arrived at for certain counts while exact numbers can be found for others.

For the Teacher: Conducting an Informal Survey

Students might inquire of parents, government officials, or science or social studies teachers for more detailed information about how such reports are handled in your area. For example, Red Cross offices are routinely called upon in disaster situations to estimate the number of people requiring help and the number actually served.

As part of the summary, ask questions to assess students' knowledge of the derivation and use of large numbers in real-world contexts.

Give some examples of numbers that you have heard reported on the news. Which of the numbers are exact? Which are estimates? Explain your answers.

How might journalists arrive at the figures they report? Use examples to explain your ideas.

Give some examples similar to those found in newspapers that make numerical comparisons between two events. How are the numbers being compared? What does the comparison tell someone about the two events?

1.2 • Aiding Hurricane Victims

This problem requires students to perform several numerical operations, helping them to review what each operation means and how and when it is used.

Launch

Open the problem by discussing the "Think about this!" question in the student edition. You may want to use a "think-pair-share" strategy for this quick exercise: give students a short time to think individually about how they might plan a relief effort and to make a few notes. Have them share and further elaborate their thinking with a partner, and then ask pairs to share their ideas with the class.

After a brief class discussion of students' ideas, have them continue to work in partners to analyze the Hurricane Andrew relief effort. You may want to put pairs of students into groups of four.

Explore

As groups explore the problem and follow-up, you may want to take this opportunity to make quick assessments of the ability of individual students to work with large numbers.

Students need to know the area of the classroom to answer part 3 of question A. Have measuring instruments available for them to make the necessary measurements. Save the classroom measurements for use in Problem 5.4, where students will need them again.

Part 4 of question A asks students how many people their classroom and their school could house. To answer this, students need to know the number of classrooms in the school and to estimate the areas of the cafeteria, gymnasium, hallways, and other rooms. Remind students to record how they arrived at their estimates; a number alone does not fully answer the question.

Part 2 of question B asks how many students are served in the school cafeteria each day. Encourage groups to make good guesses and to be able to substantiate their reasoning. You may want to check with your caterer to get an idea of how many students are actually served.

In preparation for the summary, you may want to ask groups of students to take responsibility to presenting the answer to one part of the problem. This will encourage them to organize their ideas and to listen carefully as their classmates discuss their thinking. If you choose to use this method, distribute blank transparencies, and assign one part of the problem to each group.

Summarize

Review the answers to all parts of the problem. If groups have recorded their work on transparencies, have them present their solutions to the class and, with your help, lead a class discussion about other ways to approach each question.

Part 2 of question A asks how much ground the tents would cover. If students have not realized that multiplying the number of tents by 500 allows no room for walkways, point this out yourself. A sensible estimate would probably allow, say, 600 square feet per tent, a rough estimate based on assuming a tent size of 20 feet by 25 feet and allowing 1 foot of space around each tent (or, 2 feet between tents).

For part 4 of question A, ask students to explain their estimation strategies. Some might have estimated the height and width of a typical person, used it to find an area measurement of the space needed per person, and then divided the estimated area of the classroom by the area required for a typical person.

Students will probably offer several ideas about the follow-up question. The Red Cross may have had each feeding station keep track of the number of people served. Or, the numbers may have been estimated; such estimates would have been made to order food in the first place. Or, the Red Cross may have based its estimate on the number of people in the shelters and the number of days meals were provided for them. Help the class think a bit more about this question.

> How much confidence do you have that this figure is accurate? Do you think it is close to the exact figure? Within 1000 of the exact figure?

Additional Answers

Answers to Problem 1.1

C. Possible answer: The numbers of deaths can be compared by ordering the numbers or by looking at the differences. The amounts of property damage can be compared by ordering the numbers, by using subtraction, or by dividing to find a multiple. (Some students may say that cost is difficult to compare because the disasters occurred at different times and inflation should be considered. You may want to suggest that they research how much inflation occurred during this period.)

Answers to Problem 1.2

B. 1. $250{,}000 \div 126 \approx 2000$ per station (or more, if some people receive more than one meal a day)
   2. Answers will vary.
   3. Answers will vary.
   4. $85{,}154 \div 230 \approx 370$ people per shelter

ACE Answers

Extensions

9a. Answers will vary. Students will probably choose different measures for qualifying a disaster as the "worst" of all time. One candidate is the earthquake that occurred in the Near East and eastern Mediterranean in July 1201, in which it is estimated that about 1.1 million people lost their lives. In more modern times, the highest death toll occurred in the Tangshan earthquake in eastern China on July 28, 1976, with death estimates of 242,000 to 750,000. (**Teaching Tip:** This question makes a good project or extra-credit activity. Students can do research, possibly using on-line resources, and each student or team can create a poster highlighting their discoveries. Interesting videos about disasters are also available; *National Geographic* has an excellent video entitled *Volcano.*)

9b. Possible answer: If there were one World Series earthquake a day in San Francisco, how long would it take for the death toll to equal the death toll of the earthquake of 1201? Answer: $1{,}100{,}000 \div 67 \approx 16{,}400$ days, or about 45 years.

INVESTIGATION 

Measuring Oil Spills

This investigation will help students to focus on units of measure and to develop benchmarks for common measurements, which they can in turn use to help them make sense of measurements involving large numbers.

In Problem 2.1, Describing an Oil Spill, students read an account of the *Exxon Valdez* oil spill. All numbers and associated units have been removed from the story, and students must match numbers from a list to the blanks in the story. In the process, students review common units of measure such as time, money, length, area, and volume. Problem 2.2, Finding Benchmarks for Units of Measure, offers students a more formal review of units of measure in both the customary system and the metric system and contexts in which each unit is used. In Problem 2.3, Developing a Sense of Large Numbers, students establish benchmarks to help them make sense of the data in the account of the *Exxon Valdez* oil spill.

Mathematical and Problem-Solving Goals

- *To revisit the ways that numbers are used in measurement to describe objects and events*
- *To begin building a repertoire of measurement benchmarks for use in relating measurement information to things that are personally meaningful*
- *To develop skill in using benchmark strategies, such as comparing a given figure to multiple copies of a more familiar object*

Materials

Problem	For students	For the teacher
All	Graphing calculators	Transparencies 2.1 to 2.3B (optional)
2.1	Labsheet 2.1 (optional; 1 per pair)	
2.2	Yardsticks (1 per group), stick-on notes (several per student)	Common objects to illustrate some units of measure, such as cup, pint, and quart containers; and foot rulers, yardsticks, and metersticks (optional)
2.3	Blank transparencies or large sheets of paper (optional; for sharing answers)	Almanacs or atlases

Student Pages 12–22 | Teaching the Investigation 22a–22e

2.1

Describing an Oil Spill

At a Glance

Grouping: pairs

Launch

- Introduce the news story about the *Exxon Valdez* oil spill.
- Have the class fill in the first blank or two. *(optional)*

Explore

- Have students work in pairs on the problem and in groups of four on the follow-up.

Summarize

- Have students share their choice for each blank and justify their answers.
- Review the follow-up, asking what attribute each number is measuring and whether the number is accurate or an estimate.

INVESTIGATION 2

Measuring Oil Spills

Our modern world depends on crude oil for energy and other products. As a result, huge tankers travel the world's oceans carrying oil from where it is found to where it is used. Unfortunately, some of these tankers have accidents and spill their sticky cargo on waters, beaches, and sea animals.

News reports of oil spills usually try to communicate the amount of oil spilled. Such reports may tell how many barrels were spilled, or they may give the surface area or volume of the spill. What do you think would be the best way to describe the size of an oil spill?

2.1 Describing an Oil Spill

Numbers are essential in reporting the size and effects of oil spills and in preparing for cleanup actions. To see how important numbers are, try reading this "censored" story about a famous oil spill.

> Shortly after _A_ on _B_ a giant oil tanker left Valdez, Alaska, with a load of _C_ of crude oil from the Alaskan pipeline. To avoid icebergs, the ship took a course about _D_ out of the normal shipping channel. Unfortunately, less than _E_ later the ship ran aground on the underwater Bligh Reef. The rocks of the reef tore a _F_ gash in the tanker's hull, and _G_ of crude oil spilled onto the surface of Prince William Sound. For weeks, the world watched closely as the *Exxon Valdez* oil spill became an environmental disaster, despite extensive efforts to contain and clean up the oil. The spill gradually spread to form an oil slick, covering _H_ of water and killing _I_ sea otters and _J_ birds. The cleanup engaged _K_ of boats and workers, who struggled against the cold of _L_ water and air temperatures. The cleanup cost was over _M_, including _N_ for wildlife rescue alone.

Assignment Choices

ACE questions 1, 9–11, and unassigned choices from earlier problems

Answers to Problem 2.1

Note: Students will need to reason about the size of the numbers to match them to I, J, and K, as the units of measure are given in the story rather than with the measurements.

A. 9:00 P.M.	B. March 24, 1989	C. 52,000,000 gallons
D. 2 miles	E. 3 hours	F. 600-foot
G. 10,080,000 gallons	H. 800 square miles	I. 2000 to 3000
J. 90,000 to 300,000	K. thousands	L. 40° Fahrenheit
M. $2 billion	N. $41 million	

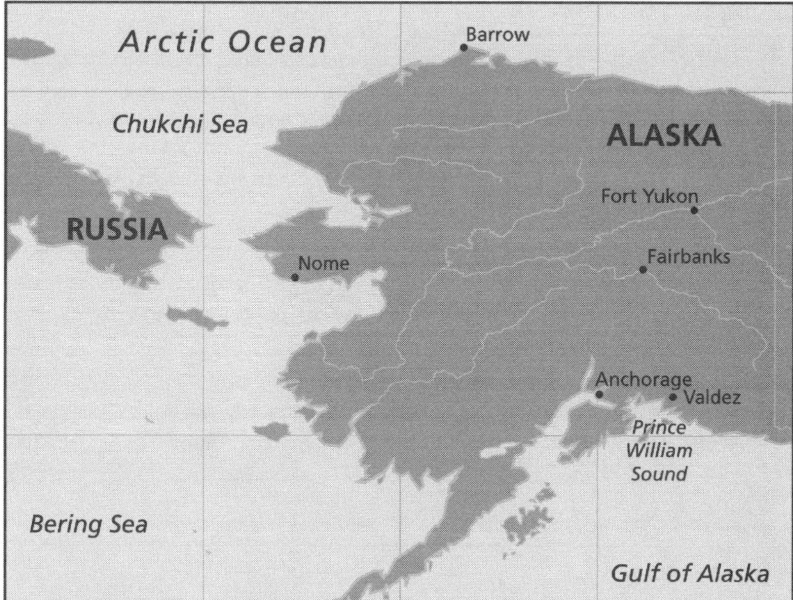

Problem 2.1

Match each lettered blank in the story with the correct measurement or range of numbers from the list below. Be prepared to explain your reasons for each choice.

800 square miles	10,080,000 gallons	$41 million
2000 to 3000	600-foot	2 miles
40° Fahrenheit	150 centimeters	90,000 to 300,000
$2 billion	March 24, 1989	52,000,000 gallons
thousands	3 hours	9:00 P.M.

Problem 2.1 Follow-Up

The numbers and measurements in Problem 2.1 describe attributes such as area, volume, and time. For example, "800 square miles" describes the area of the oil slick. You can tell that 800 square miles is an area measurement by looking at the units. Square miles are units of area. For parts A–N, describe what is being measured—for example, area, length, volume, weight, or time.

Answers to Problem 2.1 Follow-Up

A. time
B. time
C. volume
D. length
E. time
F. length
G. volume
H. area
I. number of otters
J. number of birds
K. number of boats
L. temperature
M. cost
N. cost

Finding Benchmarks for Units of Measure

At a Glance

***Grouping:* groups of 3 or 4**

Launch

- Explain that groups will be writing the names of customary and metric units on stick-on notes, and ask the class for one or two examples.

Explore

- Distribute stick-on notes, and have groups work on the problem.
- Save the follow-up until after the summary.

Summarize

- Create a class chart of the customary and metric units students found for each attribute.
- List the benchmarks students thought of for each unit.
- Have groups do the follow-up; assign question 4 as homework.

2.2 Finding Benchmarks for Units of Measure

The news report in Problem 2.1 gives measurements of time, length, area, volume, temperature, money, population, and so on. These measurements are given in two parts: a *count* and a *unit of measure.* The count tells how many units of measure are being considered. For example, 10,080,000 gallons is the volume of oil spilled. The unit of measure is gallons, and the count is 10,080,000.

To understand disaster reports in which large numbers are used, you need a sense of the size of different units of measure. You also need a sense of what large numbers "look like." For example, to imagine 10,080,000 gallons, you need a sense of "how big" a gallon is and of "how many" 10,080,000 is.

In this problem, you will develop some ***benchmarks*** to help you think about units of measure. In the United States, we use two systems of measurement. The *customary system* includes inches, gallons, and pounds. The *metric system* includes meters, liters, and grams.

Problem 2.2

This problem will help to refresh your memory of customary and metric units.

A. In your group, think of as many units of length, area, volume, weight or mass, temperature, and time as you can. Record each unit on a stick-on note. Be sure to think of both customary and metric units.

B. Group the units by the attributes they measure. Put all the units of length together, all the units of area together, and so on.

C. For each unit, try to think of something familiar that is about the size of 1 unit. For example, a sheet of notebook paper is about 1 foot long. A single-serving container of yogurt holds about 1 cup. Add each example to the stick-on note with the unit name. You can use these examples as ***benchmarks*** to help you imagine the size of something when a measurement is given.

Assignment Choices

ACE question 8 and unassigned choices from earlier problems

Answers to Problem 2.2

A, B. See the table of common units of measure given in the Summarize section.

C. Some familiar benchmarks: The top segment of the thumb is about 1 inch in length; the diameter of a quarter is about 1 inch; a paper clip has a mass of about 1 gram; the area of a football field is about 1 acre; a liter of water has a mass of about 1 kilogram.

Problem 2.2 Follow-Up

Sometimes it is convenient to know the relationship between customary and metric units of measure. The following are some common *conversions:*

1 inch = 2.54 centimeters 1 gallon ≈ 3.785 liters 1 pound ≈ 0.454 kilogram

1. **a.** Find or think of an object whose length is commonly measured in customary units. Give the length of the object in customary units, and then convert the length to metric units.
   b. Find or think of an object whose length is commonly measured in metric units. Give the length of the object in metric units, and then convert the length to customary units.
2. **a.** Find or think of an object whose volume is commonly measured in customary units. Give the volume of the object in customary units, and then convert the volume to metric units.
   b. Find or think of an object whose volume is commonly measured in metric units. Give the volume of the object in metric units, and then convert the volume to customary units.

Did you know?

Ounces and pounds are measures of weight. *Weight* is the force with which an object is attracted toward Earth (or some other body). Grams and kilograms are measures of mass. *Mass* is a measure of the amount of material an object contains. If you stood on the Moon, you would have the same mass that you have on Earth. However, since the gravitational pull of the Moon is weaker than that of Earth, you would weigh less on the Moon than you do on Earth. For measurements made on Earth, the distinction between mass and weight is not critical, and the terms are often used interchangeably.

3. **a.** Find or think of an object whose weight is commonly measured in customary units. Give the weight of the object in customary units, and then convert this measurement to metric units.
   b. Find or think of an object whose mass is commonly measured in metric units. Give the mass of the object in metric units, and then convert this measurement to customary units.
4. Find three items in your home or school that are labeled with both customary and metric units.

Answers to Problem 2.2 Follow-Up

1. a. Possible answer: In the United States, people commonly measure their height in feet and inches. A person 5 feet 2 inches tall is $62 \times 2.54 = 157.48$ centimeters tall.
   b. Possible answer: In Canada, height is commonly measured in centimeters. A person 170 centimeters tall is $170 \div 2.54 \approx 67$ inches, or 5 feet 7 inches, tall.
2. a. Possible answer: Milk is commonly measured in quarts, and 1 quart ≈ 0.946 liter.
   b. In Canada, gas is commonly measured in liters, and 1 liter ≈ 0.264 gallon.
3. a. Possible answer: Butter is typically measured in pounds, and 1 pound ≈ 454 grams.
   b. In chemistry, materials are typically measured in grams, and 1 gram ≈ 0.035 ounce.
4. Possible answer: thermometers, food items, and cleaning products

Developing a Sense of Large Numbers

At a Glance

Grouping: groups of 4

Launch

- Read the problem introduction, and do part A as a class activity. (*optional*)

Explore

- Groups may work individually on the parts of the problem but should agree on each comparison.
- Distribute transparencies or large sheets of paper for groups to record answers. (*optional*)

Summarize

- Have each group offer their comparison for one part, and allow the class to discuss it and add their own ideas.
- Assign the follow-up, having students think about it individually and then share ideas in their groups.

2.3 Developing a Sense of Large Numbers

You can imagine what a gallon of oil looks like, but can you imagine 10,080,000 gallons spread over 800 square miles of Prince William Sound? You have a sense of how long a foot is, but can you picture a 600-foot gash in the hull of an oil tanker? You know the value of $1, but can you imagine the value of the $41 million spent rescuing wildlife from the *Exxon Valdez* oil spill?

One way to understand measurements with large numbers is to find something familiar that is the same size. For example, Los Angeles and New York City have a combined land area of just about 800 square miles. The *Exxon Valdez* oil slick would have nearly covered those two cities.

Another way to make sense of measurements with large numbers is to think about copies of something familiar. For example, an American football field is 300 feet long (without the end zones). The gash in the *Exxon Valdez* was as long as two football fields. Operating America's public schools costs an average of $4500 per student each year. The money spent on the *Exxon Valdez* wildlife rescue is equal to the cost of school for more than 9000 students—or all the seventh graders in Alaska!

Did you know?

The immediate impact of the *Exxon Valdez* oil spill on the marine wildlife in coastal Alaska was tremendous. Within two months of the disaster, cleanup crews had retrieved over 35,000 dead birds from the state's oily shorelines. Biologists estimate that a total of about 250,000 birds were killed by the spill. One species, the marbled murrelet, lost an amazing 30 percent of its native population. Fortunately, as the Alaskan ecosystem slowly heals, seabird colonies have been returning to their earlier population levels.

Assignment Choices

ACE questions 2–7 and unassigned choices from earlier problems

Answers to Problem 2.3

A possible answer is given for each part.

A. The oil spilled by the *Exxon Valdez* would fill more than 20 Olympic-size swimming pools.

B. The tanker was so far off course that if it were aiming at the U.S. Capitol, it would have instead hit the White House, about 2 miles away.

C. The water and air temperatures during the cleanup were close to that of our estuary last January 1, when people jumped in the water to celebrate New Year's Day. They had to get out of the water immediately and dry off or risk serious injury.

D. In less time than it takes to play a typical baseball or football game, the tanker had run aground on Bligh Reef.

Problem 2.3

In parts A–G, facts about the *Exxon Valdez* disaster are given. Imagine you are a newspaper reporter assigned to the story. Use your own ideas or the hints given to write statements communicating each fact in a way that would be easy for your readers to understand.

A. *The* Exxon Valdez *spilled 10,080,000 gallons of crude oil.*
Hint: An Olympic-size swimming pool holds about 500,000 gallons of water. How many such pools could be filled with the 10,080,000 gallons of oil?

B. *The tanker strayed about 2 miles out of the usual shipping channel.*
Hint: What places in your area are about 2 miles apart?

C. *The water and air temperatures during the oil spill cleanup were about 40° Fahrenheit.*
Hint: When, if ever, do the water and air temperatures in your area reach these temperatures? Do you go swimming then?

D. *The tanker ran aground on Bligh Reef less than 3 hours after it left port.*
Hint: What familiar events last about 3 hours?

E. *The oil spill killed 90,000 to 300,000 seabirds.*
Hint: Consult an almanac or atlas to find cities or towns in your state with human populations about this size.

F. *The entire cleanup operation cost $2,000,000,000.*
Hint: In the United States, the mean annual pay for workers is about $25,000. How many annual salaries could be paid from the cleanup cost of the oil spill?

G. *The oil slick eventually covered 800 square miles of the ocean's surface.*
Hint: 1 mile is 5280 feet, so 1 square mile is 5280 × 5280 = 27,878,400 square feet. Estimate the area of your classroom floor. Then, figure out how many such classroom floors it would take to cover 1 square mile and to cover the 800-square-mile oil slick.

E. Estimates of the number of seabirds killed by the oil spill range from 90,000—about the population of Gainesville, Florida—to 300,000—about the population of Tampa.

F. The cost of the cleanup was $2,000,000,000, about equal to the average annual pay of 80,000 U.S. workers.

G. For classrooms measuring 25 feet by 40 feet, 1 square mile would cover 27,878,400 ÷ 1000 ≈ 28,000 classrooms. Therefore, the 800-square-mile oil slick would cover roughly 28,000 × 800 = 22,400,000 classrooms. Also, the oil slick would cover more than 500,000 football fields.

Problem 2.3 Follow-Up

The *Exxon Valdez* oil tanker was 987 feet long. You can get a sense of this length by imagining a "human chain."

1. Make an estimate of the arm span, in feet, of a typical seventh grader. Figure out how many seventh graders it would take to stretch out in a line as long as the *Exxon Valdez.*

2. Would the chain require more students than are in your class? Would it require more students than are in your school?
3. Would this chain fit in the hall of your school? Would it fit across the football field or soccer field?

Answers to Problem 2.3 Follow-Up

1. The arm span of a typical seventh grader is about 5 feet, so it would take about 197 students standing in a line to equal the length of the tanker.
2. The chain would require more students than are in a typical math class and may or may not require more students than are in the school.
3. It is unlikely that a human chain the length of the tanker would fit in a school hallway. It would cover about three football fields and would probably be longer than the school soccer field as well.

Applications • Connections • Extensions

As you work on these ACE questions, use your calculator whenever you need it.

Applications

In 1–6, use the following information: On May 18, 1980, Mount St. Helens, a volcano in southwestern Washington, erupted with a blast of hot gas and rock that devastated more than **150,000 acres** of prime timberland and sent a mushroom cloud of ash **90,000 feet** into the atmosphere and then around the world. The blast triggered the largest landslide in recorded history—**4 billion cubic yards** of shattered rock poured down the mountainside at a speed of **17,600 feet per minute.** The Mount St. Helens eruption killed **60 people** and caused an estimated **$970 million** in damage. When the main eruption was over, the mountain had lost **1313 feet** from its original height of **9677 feet.**

1. Tell which of the boldface measurements are measures of the given attribute.

a. length **b.** area **c.** volume **d.** weight or mass

e. money **f.** speed **g.** temperature **h.** population

2. The Washington Monument is 550 feet tall. How many such monuments would be needed to make a tower reaching to the top of the Mount St. Helens ash cloud?

3. Glenn Robinson, the Milwaukee Bucks basketball star, earns about $6 million per year. How many years of his salary would be needed to pay for the damage from the Mount St. Helens eruption?

Answers

Applications

1a. 90,000 feet, 1313 feet, 9677 feet

1b. 150,000 acres

1c. 4 billion cubic yards

1d. No data describe weight or mass.

1e. $970 million

1f. 17,600 feet per minute

1g. No data describe temperature.

1h. 60 people

2. $90{,}000 \div 550 \approx 164$ monuments

3. $970 \div 6 \approx 162$ years

4. 970,000,000 ÷ 16,300 ≈ 59,500 salaries

5. 150,000 ÷ 2 = 75,000 fields

6. Using subtraction or division, students can make several comparative statements; a few are offered here.

6a. If four Superdomes were stacked on top of one another, they would reach a height approximately equal to the height lost from the peak of Mount St. Helens (1313 ÷ 350 ≈ 3.75). The height lost from the peak is about 1313 – 350 = 963 feet more than the height of the Superdome. The area destroyed by the blast is equal to the ground covered by more than 150,000 ÷ 13 ≈ 11,500 Superdomes.

6b. The rock pouring down the side of Mount St. Helens traveled a little more than three times the speed of a car traveling at 65 miles per hour (17,600 ÷ 5720 ≈ 3).

6c. The Mount St. Helens eruption caused almost as many deaths as the 1989 earthquake.

7. Possible answers: A midsize car weighs about 2 tons, so it would take about 600,000 tons ÷ 2 tons = 300,000 midsize cars to balance the platform. A ton is 2000 pounds, and a typical seventh grader weighs 100 pounds, so it would take about 12,000,000 students to equal the weight of the platform.

4. The median annual salary per worker in the United States in 1983 was about $16,300. About how many such salaries would it take to pay for the damage from the Mount St. Helens eruption?

5. The playing field in a major league baseball park covers about 2 acres of land. How many such fields would it take to cover the timberland destroyed by the Mount St. Helens eruption?

6. Use the given facts as benchmark data to write statements for a news report describing the size and effects of the Mount St. Helens eruption.

a. The Louisiana Superdome is the largest sports arena in the world. It covers 13 acres and reaches a height of about 350 feet.

b. A car traveling 65 miles per hour moves 5720 feet per minute.

c. Sixty-seven deaths were caused by the San Francisco earthquake of October 17, 1989.

7. An offshore oil platform, Hibernia, is being built 200 miles off the coast of Newfoundland. It will weigh 600,000 tons, making it the heaviest such platform in the world. Develop a benchmark to help you make sense of the weight of this platform.

Connections

8. Tell what customary and metric units you could use to measure the following things. For example, for a television set, you could measure the length, width, or diagonal of the screen in inches or centimeters; you could measure the weight or mass in pounds or kilograms; and you could measure the area of the screen in square inches or square centimeters.

a. a car

b. a contact lens

c. a trip from Boston to Seattle

d. a house or an apartment

e. the water used in your school each day

Connections

8. A possible answer is given for each item.

8a. You could measure the length, width, or height of a car in feet or meters, and the weight or mass in pounds, tons, or kilograms.

8b. You could measure the diameter or thickness of a contact lens in fractions of inches or millimeters, and the weight or mass in fractions of ounces or grams.

8c. You could measure the length of a trip from Boston to Seattle in miles or kilometers or in terms of time, using hours for an air trip and days for a car trip.

8d. You could measure the size of a house or an apartment in terms of numbers of rooms or square feet or square meters of floor space, and the height of the ceilings in feet or meters.

8e. You could measure the water use in gallons or liters.

9. When oil began leaking from the *Exxon Valdez,* cleanup teams tried to contain the spill by surrounding it with floating booms. Before the slick could be contained, the oil spread too far for the supply of boom sections.

   a. Suppose you have 20,000 meters of boom sections to arrange in the shape of a rectangle. Of all the rectangles you could make from the boom sections, which rectangle would have the greatest area? Give the dimensions and the area of the rectangle.

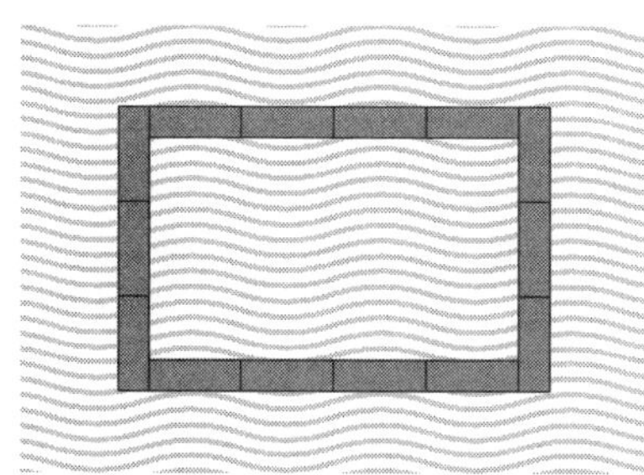

   b. Suppose you can arrange 20,000 meters of flexible boom sections in any shape you choose. Which shape could contain the greatest oil slick area?

Extensions

In 10 and 11, use the following information: In terms of gallons of oil spilled, there have been spills larger than the *Exxon Valdez* disaster. On July 19, 1979, two tankers collided near the islands of Trinidad and Tobago, releasing 88,200,000 gallons of crude oil into the Caribbean Sea. On June 3, 1979, an oil well in the Gulf of Mexico exploded and spilled 180,000,000 gallons of crude oil before it was capped.

10. Compare the *Exxon Valdez* disaster with these two spills.

11. If you were writing a news report on these spills, what other measures of damage would you want to include?

9a. The rectangle that would contain the greatest area is a square 5000 meters on each side. It would have an area of 25,000,000 square meters.

9b. A circle of circumference 20,000 meters would contain the greatest area, which would be $\pi(3180)^2$, or approximately 32,000,000, square meters.

Extensions

10. The *Exxon Valdez* spilled about 10,080,000 gallons of crude oil, which is about $\frac{1}{9}$ of the Trinidad and Tobago spill and about $\frac{1}{18}$ of the Gulf of Mexico spill.

11. Possible answer: cleanup cost, damage to wildlife, miles of beach affected, dollar value of oil lost, loss of earning potential of local businesses

Possible Answers

1. *Length:* inch, foot, yard, mile, millimeter, centimeter, meter, kilometer; *Area:* square inch, square mile, acre, square centimeter, square meter, square kilometer; *Volume:* cubic inch, cup, pint, quart, gallon, cubic centimeter, liter; *Weight or mass:* ounce, pound, ton, gram, kilogram; *Temperature:* Fahrenheit, Celsius; *Time:* second, minute, hour, day, week, year, decade, century

2. *Length:* mile—distance from my house to school, inch—about the length of the top segment of my thumb, centimeter—the diameter of the head of a large tack; *Area:* square foot—area of one of the tiles on the classroom floor, acre—about the area of a football field; *Volume:* liter—half the volume of a 2-liter soft drink container; *Mass:* gram—the mass of a small paper clip; *Temperature:* Celsius—water freezes at 0° and boils at 100°; *Time:* hour—length of math class

3. One strategy for understanding measurements containing large numbers is to find a familiar object with the same measurement. You could also determine the number of copies of some smaller benchmark that would equal the given measurement.

Mathematical Reflections

In this investigation, you reviewed customary and metric units of measure. You also practiced some useful strategies for making sense of disaster reports that include large numbers and many different units. These questions will help you summarize what you have learned:

1. What are some common units for measuring length, area, volume, weight or mass, temperature, and time?
2. What familiar things could you use as benchmarks to explain to someone the sizes of the units you listed in question 1? Select one or two units of measure for each type of measurement (length, area, volume, and so on), and give an example of a benchmark for each.
3. What are some strategies you can use to better understand the size of something that is expressed by a measurement with a very large number?

Think about your answers to these questions, discuss your ideas with other students and your teacher, and then write a summary of your findings in your journal.

Tips for the Linguistically Diverse Classroom

Original Rebus The Original Rebus technique is described in detail in *Getting to Know Connected Mathematics*. Students make a copy of the text before it is discussed. During the discussion, they generate their own rebuses for words they do not understand; the words are made comprehensible through pictures, objects, or demonstrations. Example: Question 1—Key words for which students might make rebuses are *length* (line), *area* (rectangle with interior shaded), *volume* (container), *weight* or *mass* (scale), *temperature* (thermometer), *time* (clock).

TEACHING THE INVESTIGATION

2.1 • Describing an Oil Spill

In this problem, students read an account of the *Exxon Valdez* oil spill. All of the numerical data and units have been deleted from the story, giving students an opportunity to think about what sorts of measurement units and amounts make sense in specific contexts. Students are to match the numbers in a list to the blanks in the story. The units of measure serve as clues to how the measurements and numbers are related.

Launch

Introduce the news story. You may want to have the class fill in the first blank or two (on Transparency 2.1, if possible) to verify that they understand the process.

Explore

This problem is best done by pairs of students. You may want to distribute a copy of Labsheet 2.1 to each pair of students. When pairs are finished, have them meet in groups of four to discuss their answers and then work on the follow-up.

Summarize

Display Transparency 2.1 again, and call on students to fill in the blanks in the story. To make this exercise effective, it is important to ask students to justify each selection. If there is disagreement, give students time to explain their decision, while others either agree or explain why they think the answers are incorrect.

Discuss the follow-up, which foreshadows the topic of Problem 2.2. For each blank in the story, ask these questions:

> What attribute is this number measuring?
>
> Is this number accurate, or is it an estimate? Why do you think so?

2.2 • Finding Benchmarks for Units of Measure

We must be able to appreciate the unit of measure attached to a particular number for the number to have meaning for us. This problem will clarify for students the units, both customary and metric, associated with various measurement tasks. Students brainstorm a list of common units of measure, group them by the attribute measured (such as length, area, or time), and think of some common examples, or *benchmarks,* for each unit.

Launch

Explain to the class that they will be trying to think of as many different units of measure as they can, in both customary and metric (or international) units. Give them an attribute, such as length, and ask for examples of customary and metric units that could be used to measure that attribute. Write each unit on a stick-on note.

Begin a table on the board similar to the one below.

Attribute	Customary units	Metric units	Benchmark
length	inch foot	centimeter	

Ask the class:

> Which unit would you use to measure your height? Which unit would you use to measure the distance from this classroom to the gym?

Leave students with the following questions to think about as they explore Problem 2.2:

> What is something familiar to you that is about the size of 1 foot? About the size of 1 inch? About the size of 1 centimeter? We will add your examples to our chart later.

Have students gather in groups of three or four to work on the problem.

Save the follow-up for after the summary of the problem. Some students know that cups, pints, and quarts are common units of measure but don't have a real sense of their size. Having some measuring containers availabe in the classroom may be helpful.

Explore

Distribute stick-on notes to each group. Have groups write on their notes and sort their information at their table. Wait until all groups are finished before adding more entries to the class chart.

As groups work, verify that they are addressing each of the attributes listed in part A.

Summarize

Summarize the class's findings by asking for the units of measure the students found for each of the given attributes. You might have one group present their ideas first, and then ask other groups to add units that the first group did not list. Add the units of measure to the class chart. The completed chart might look like this:

<table>
<tr><th>Attribute</th><th>Customary units</th><th>Metric units</th><th>Benchmark</th></tr>
<tr><td>length</td><td>inch
foot
yard
mile</td><td>millimeter
centimeter
meter
kilometer</td><td></td></tr>
<tr><td>area</td><td>square inch
square foot
square yard
square mile
acre</td><td>square centimeter
square meter
square kilometer
hectare</td><td></td></tr>
<tr><td>volume</td><td>cubic inch
cubic foot
cubic yard
cup
pint
quart
gallon</td><td>cubic centimeter
cubic meter
liter</td><td></td></tr>
<tr><td>weight or mass</td><td>ounce
pound
ton</td><td>milligram
gram
kilogram</td><td></td></tr>
<tr><td>temperature</td><td>degree Fahrenheit</td><td>degree Celsius</td><td></td></tr>
<tr><td>time</td><td colspan="2">second
minute
hour
day
week
century</td><td></td></tr>
</table>

Once all of the ideas are listed, help students to think about benchmarks for measurements and how they might be used.

What makes a good benchmark? *(something common or familiar)*

Now, ask students to offer the benchmarks they thought of for each unit, and add these ideas to the class chart.

Some people use these benchmarks to help them estimate measurements. For example, a friend of mine uses the width of one of her fingernails to estimate 1 centimeter when she is measuring short lengths.

Of the benchmarks listed for each unit, which works best in what kinds of situations? Why?

How might you use one of these benchmarks to estimate the size of your math book? The length of this classroom? The distance from this classroom to the cafeteria? The weight of your chair?

Have the class read through the follow-up, and work through part a of question 1 as a class. Then, have students work in their groups on the rest of question 1 and on questions 2 and 3.

When everyone is finished, have groups share their work. Be sure students explain how they converted the units. Follow-up question 4 could be assigned as homework and discussed at the start of the next class.

2.3 • Developing a Sense of Large Numbers

Students' work in this problem will help them to further develop their ability to make sense of measurements involving large numbers. Students write statements about facts containing large numbers, either directly comparing the numbers to something more familiar or comparing them to benchmarks consisting of multiples of a familiar object or event—for example, the 600-foot gash made in the hull of the *Exxon Valdez* is about equal to the length of two football fields.

Launch

Students will need almanacs or atlases with information for their state for part E of the problem. You may want to gather these resources beforehand.

Read the introduction to the problem with the class. You may want to do part A as a class to model what is expected. Give everyone a minute to think about the statement, and then have a class discussion on the various ideas. Have students work on the problem in groups of four.

Explore

Groups may want to do one part together and then assign the remaining parts to individual group members; however, the entire group should review and reach an agreement about each comparison.

You may want to distribute transparencies or large sheets of paper for groups to record their final comparisons for all seven parts for sharing in the summary.

Save the follow-up questions for the summary.

Summarize

Ask a different group to share their statements for each part of the problem, and allow time for discussion. Encourage the class to consider the reasonableness of each group's examples, and allow other groups to add interesting statements that are different from those of the group reporting. If students have recorded their answers on transparencies or large sheet of papers, display them for everyone to examine.

After the discussion of the problem, assign the follow-up. Give students a few minutes to think about the problem on their own, and then have them gather in their groups to discuss their ideas. Each group will need to determine a typical student's arm span.

Have students share their solutions and explain how they estimated a typical student's arm span. Verify that students understand that their estimated arm span is their benchmark and that they know how to use this benchmark to make sense of the ship's length.

Comparing Large Numbers

In the data-rich problems in this investigation, students review and refine their skills in reading, writing, ordering, and interpreting large numbers. They also continue to develop ways to compare large numbers.

Problem 3.1, Playing Dialing Digits, is a hands-on activity that asks students to think about strategies for playing a game that is based on the concept of place value. Problem 3.2, Getting Things in Order, asks students to order the 20 largest U.S. metropolitan areas by population and then to order the cities associated with the metropolitan areas by population. In their work with the numerical data, students also have an opportunity to think critically about geography. In Problem 3.3, Rounding Numbers, students think about appropriate degrees of accuracy in relation to the rounding of large numbers. In Problem 3.4, Comparing Hog Populations, students compare domestic swine populations in North Carolina counties over a ten-year interval both by comparing population figures directly and by comparing percent change over the time span.

Mathematical and Problem-Solving Goals

- *To read and write large numbers*
- *To round numbers and to make judgments about the degree of accuracy of numbers*
- *To compare large numbers by ordering and with rates*

Materials

Problem	For students	For the teacher
All	Graphing calculators	Transparencies 3.1 to 3.4 (optional)
3.1	Labsheet 3.1A (1 per pair or group), Labsheet 3.1B (1 per student or pair), bobby pins or paper clips (for making spinners; 1 per group)	Transparency of Labsheet 3.1A (optional)
3.2	Labsheet 3.2 (1 per group), almanacs or U.S. maps	Transparency of Labsheet 3.2 (optional), large U.S. map (optional)

Student Pages 23–37 Teaching the Investigation 37a–37h

Comparing Large Numbers

You have seen that the numbers used to report the size of natural disasters and accidents are often very large. Hurricane Andrew caused $20 billion in property damage; the *Exxon Valdez* oil slick covered about 22,300,000,000 square feet of ocean surface; and the Mount St. Helens eruption blasted 4 billion cubic yards of rock off the top of the mountain. To solve problems about situations like these and to discuss your results with others, you need to know how to write and read large numbers.

The standard notation for writing numbers involves ten digits—0, 1, 2, 3, 4, 5, 6, 7, 8, and 9—and a *place-value system.* To write and read numbers greater than 999, we group the places into clusters of three.

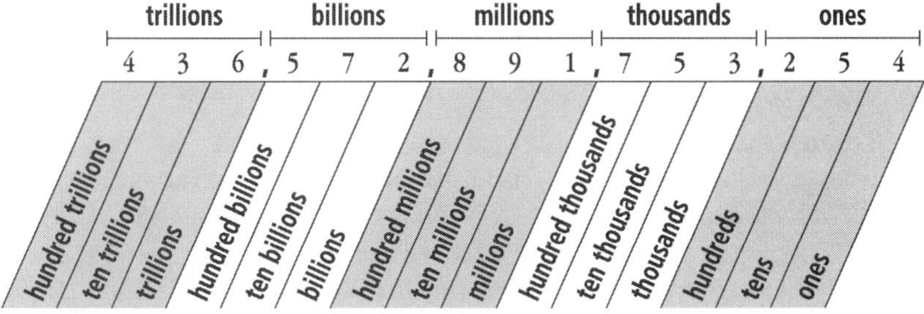

The number 436,572,891,753,254 is read "four hundred thirty-six *trillion,* five hundred seventy-two *billion,* eight hundred ninety-one *million,* seven hundred fifty-three *thousand,* two hundred fifty-four." Notice that in this number the digit 2 appears in two places. In one place, it stands for two billion; in the other place, it stands for two hundred.

Playing Dialing Digits

At a Glance

Grouping: small groups

Launch

- Offer a large number for students to read.
- Introduce the game, and demonstrate a couple of turns.
- Distribute a spinner and game cards to each player or team.

Explore

- Circulate as students play the game, reminding them to record any winning strategies they discover.

Summarize

- Let students share the strategies they found.
- Raise the issue of probability as it relates to the game.
- Have teams play one of the variations in the follow-up and talk about winning strategies.

3.1 Playing Dialing Digits

You can test your skill in reading, writing, and comparing numbers by playing the Dialing Digits game.

Rules for Dialing Digits

Dialing Digits is played by two or more players or teams.

Materials

- Pencils
- Dialing Digits spinner
- Dialing Digits game cards (1 per player)

On the Dialing Digits game card, the blanks for each game represent place values for a nine-digit number.

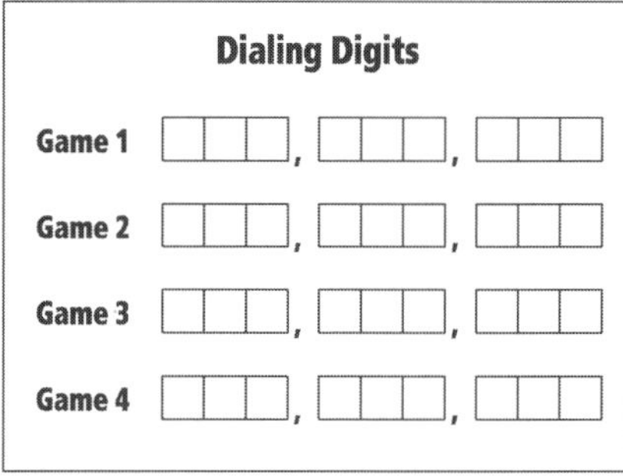

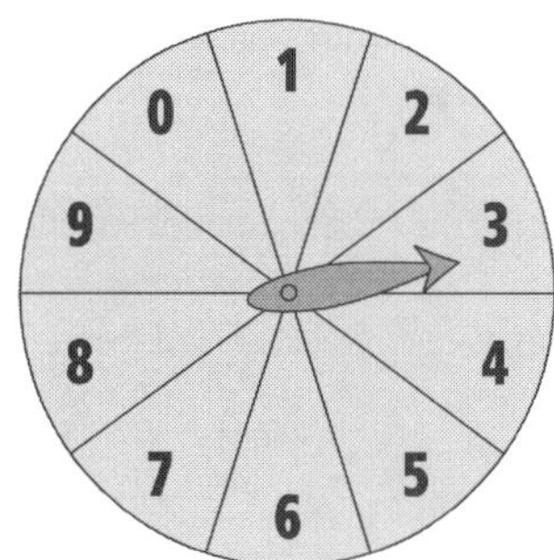

Directions

- Players take turns spinning the spinner. After each spin, each player must write the digit spun in one of the empty blanks for that game. Players should keep their game cards hidden from each other until the end of the game.
- The game proceeds until all the blanks have been filled. The player that has placed the digits to make the greatest number wins. However, before earning the win, the player must correctly read the number that has been produced.

Problem 3.1

Play Dialing Digits several times with different opponents. Record any strategies you find that help you win.

Assignment Choices

ACE questions 1, 2, 8, 12, and unassigned choices from earlier problems

Answer to Problem 3.1

Strategies will vary. In general, greater numbers should be placed toward the left and smaller numbers toward the right. Students may also mention the role of probability in their playing strategies.

Problem 3.1 Follow-Up

You can vary Dialing Digits to make it more challenging. Here are two variations:

- Play two rounds of the game, and have each player add his or her numbers for the two rounds. The player with the greatest sum wins.
- Play two rounds of the game, and have each player subtract the number for round 2 from the number for round 1. The team with the greatest difference wins.

Play Dialing Digits again, using one of these variations. Describe a strategy for winning.

3.2 Getting Things in Order

You have seen that reports of natural disasters often involve large numbers. Large numbers also occur frequently in population data. The table below shows 1992 populations of the 20 largest metropolitan areas in the United States. A *metropolitan area* consists of a central city and smaller surrounding communities.

Metropolitan area	Population
Atlanta	2,959,950
Boston	5,455,403
Chicago	8,239,820
Cleveland	2,859,644
Dallas	4,037,282
Detroit	5,187,171
Houston	3,731,131
Los Angeles	14,531,529
Miami	3,192,582
Minneapolis	2,538,834
New York City	19,549,649
Philadelphia	5,892,937
Phoenix	2,238,480
Pittsburgh	2,394,811
St. Louis	2,492,525
San Diego	2,498,016
San Francisco	6,253,311
Seattle	2,970,328
Tampa	2,067,959
Washington, D.C.	6,727,050

Source: U.S. Bureau of the Census, as reported in *The World Almanac and Book of Facts 1996.* Ed. Robert Famighetti. Mahwah, New Jersey: Funk and Wagnalls, 1995.

3.2 Getting Things in Order

At a Glance

***Grouping:* groups of 2 or 3**

Launch

- Read through the problem with the class.
- Have groups work on the problem and follow-up.

Explore

- Ask each student to keep a record of the answers.
- Supply maps or other resources if needed for part C.

Summarize

- Review the ranking of the metropolitan areas, and ask how students ordered them.
- Display a U.S. map, and help the class locate each area and label it with its rank.
- Talk about why the areas are where they are and how their locations affect government and business decisions.
- Discuss the follow-up.

Answer to Problem 3.1 Follow-Up

Strategies will vary. In general, both numbers in the sum game should be as large as possible. In the difference game, the first number should be as large as possible, and the second number should be as small as possible.

Assignment Choices

ACE questions 3, 4, 11, and unassigned choices from earlier problems

Problem 3.2

The census data are given in alphabetical order, but it is often interesting and important to look at *ranking* by size. An increase in population can bring greater political and economic power to an area.

A. Order the 20 metropolitan areas from most populated to least populated.

B. Describe some ways you could compare the populations of these metropolitan areas.

C. Locate each of the 20 metropolitan areas on the U.S. map on Labsheet 3.2. Look for interesting patterns in the locations of these areas.

1. What geographic factors seem to lead to large population centers?
2. How do you think the locations of these large metropolitan areas affect national and state government and business decisions?

Problem 3.2 Follow-Up

1. The table on the next page shows the population of the major city in each metropolitan area. List the cities in order from most populated to least populated.
2. Compare the ranking for the cities to the ranking for the metropolitan areas. Give some possible reasons for any differences you find.

Answers to Problem 3.2

A. New York City, Los Angeles, Chicago, Washington, D.C., San Francisco, Philadelphia, Boston, Detroit, Dallas, Houston, Miami, Seattle, Atlanta, Cleveland, Minneapolis, San Diego, St. Louis, Pittsburgh, Phoenix, Tampa

B. Answers will vary. Students can compare the populations by computing differences or ratios.

C. 1. Possible answer: Metropolitan areas tend to be located near coasts or along rivers and not in deserts or mountainous areas.

2. Possible answer: Governments would consider the location of large metropolitan areas when they decide where to put new interstate highways and airports or where to concentrate on repairs and upgrades to existing structures. Businesses would consider the location of large metropolitan areas when they decide where to build things like manufacturing plants and retail outlets.

Metropolitan area	Population of metropolitan area	Population of city
Atlanta	2,959,950	393,929
Boston	5,455,403	574,283
Chicago	8,239,820	2,783,726
Cleveland	2,859,644	505,616
Dallas	4,037,282	1,007,618
Detroit	5,187,171	1,027,974
Houston	3,731,131	1,629,902
Los Angeles	14,531,529	3,485,557
Miami	3,192,582	358,648
Minneapolis	2,538,834	368,383
New York City	19,549,649	7,322,564
Philadelphia	5,892,937	1,585,577
Phoenix	2,238,480	983,403
Pittsburgh	2,394,811	369,879
St. Louis	2,492,525	396,685
San Diego	2,498,016	1,110,554
San Francisco	6,253,311	723,959
Seattle	2,970,328	516,259
Tampa	2,067,959	280,015
Washington, D.C.	6,727,050	606,900

Source: U.S. Bureau of the Census, as reported in *The World Almanac and Book of Facts 1996.* Ed. Robert Famighetti. Mahwah, New Jersey: Funk and Wagnalls, 1995.

Did you know?

With more than half the state's automobile and human populations, New York City has its share of cleaning to do. While people may complain about how dirty the city is, the streets today are spotless compared to 150 years ago. Before the first sewer systems were built during the nineteenth century, New York City streets were so filthy that herds of abandoned farm hogs roamed the city, eating the trash that piled up along the roadside. During his visit to the city in 1842, British author Charles Dickens joked that New Yorkers ought to "take care of the pigs, for they are the city scavengers." Today, structural engineers face the difficult task of renovating old-fashioned sewer systems without disturbing the bustling businesses of America's largest city.

Answers to Problem 3.2 Follow-Up

1. New York City, Los Angeles, Chicago, Houston, Philadelphia, San Diego, Detroit, Dallas, Phoenix, San Francisco, Washington, D.C., Boston, Seattle, Cleveland, St. Louis, Atlanta, Pittsburgh, Minneapolis, Miami, Tampa
2. The three largest metropolitan areas (New York City, Los Angeles, and Chicago) and the smallest (Tampa) are the same as the city ranking; except for Cleveland, the order of all the other metropolitan areas differs from the city ranking. This might be because most of the population of the three largest metropolitan areas is concentrated in the city itself, and the other metropolitan areas include many more smaller suburbs.

Rounding Numbers

At a Glance

***Grouping:* pairs**

Launch

- Discuss the problem introduction with the class.
- Have students work in pairs on the problem and follow-up.

Explore

- If pairs struggle with the problem, have them do the follow-up first.
- As pairs work on the follow-up, look for interesting ways they reason about how to round the population figures.

Summarize

- Have several pairs share their answers and reasoning for each part of the problem.
- Talk about the follow-up and how students rounded the figures.

3.3 Rounding Numbers

The census data in Problem 3.2 are given as exact counts, but since exact populations are difficult to calculate and change daily, populations are often given as rounded figures. For example, the population of the Los Angeles metropolitan area might be rounded as shown:

Actual count (1992)	14,531,529
Rounded to the nearest ten million	10,000,000
Rounded to the nearest million	15,000,000
Rounded to the nearest hundred thousand	14,500,000

By using rounded numbers, you can give a general idea of size without claiming exactness. And, most people find it easier to think about and compare numbers with fewer non-zero digits. When you round a number, you need to consider the situation in order to decide how accurate the rounded number should be.

Problem 3.3

In 1990, the population of the United States was reported to be 248,709,873. Here are four possible roundings of this number:

200,000,000 250,000,000 249,000,000 248,700,000

A. The population of the world is about 5.7 billion. Which of the above roundings would you use if you wanted to compare the population of the United States with the population of the world? Give reasons for your choice.

B. The population of India is about 1 billion. Which rounding would you use if you wanted to compare the population of the United States with the population of India? Give reasons for your choice.

C. In 1980, the population of the United States was about 226,000,000. Which rounding would you use if you wanted to compare the 1990 U.S. population with this 1980 population figure? Give reasons for your choice.

Problem 3.3 Follow-Up

Look again at the list of the 20 largest metropolitan areas. Round these population figures in a way that makes sense to you. Explain your reasoning. Do your roundings preserve the original ranking? Why or why not?

Assignment Choices

ACE questions 6, 7, 9, 13, 16–19, and unassigned choices from earlier problems (It is common to see large numbers in the abbreviated form used in 13, so we highly recommend assigning it. It also makes a good group activity.)

Answers to Problem 3.3

A. Possible answer: The 200,000,000 figure is probably close enough to give a general idea of the relationship between the U.S. population and the world population.

B. Possible answer: The 250,000,000 figure is probably better than the 200,000,000 figure because it shows a more accurate 4:1 ratio than the 5:1 ratio indicated by the 200,000,000 figure.

C. Possible answer: The 249,000,000 figure is rounded to the nearest million, as is 226,000,000, so it is probably the best choice.

Answer to Problem 3.3 Follow-Up

Possible answer: I rounded the numbers to the nearest ten thousand so that they would stay in the same order. (Students should include a list of the rounded numbers.)

3.4 Comparing Hog Populations

In areas with large populations of people or animals, finding ways to dispose of waste can be a problem. Any area must deal with the storage, treatment, and disposal of garbage and hazardous chemical wastes. Areas with industries involving great numbers of animals must also deal with the treatment and disposal of animal wastes.

Did you know?

In 1995, at a hog farm in northern Onslow County, North Carolina, the walls of an 8-acre wastewater lagoon collapsed. Within an hour, 25 million gallons of raw hog waste had poured through a 25-foot-wide breech in the 12-foot wall into a nearby river. Over the next few days, the wastewater swirled downstream, smothering and suffocating more than 3500 fish.

Hog farming is an important business in North Carolina. In fact, one area of the state, shown in dark orange on the map below, is known as the "hog belt."

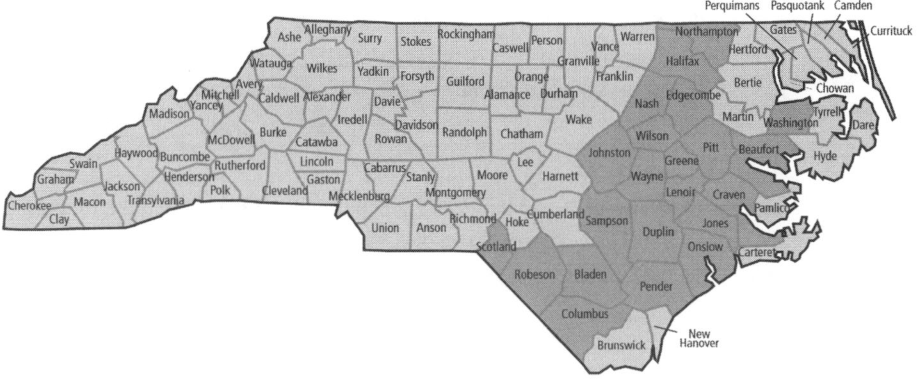

Comparing Hog Populations

At a Glance

Grouping:* *pairs

Launch

- Talk with the class about the Onslow County disaster.
- Have the class study the table of hog data.
- Have students work in pairs on the problem and follow-up.

Explore

- Circulate as pairs write comparison statements.
- If all the statements a pair writes are of the same type, ask for another kind of statement.

Summarize

- Have pairs get together to share their comparisons with each other and then with the class.
- Review the follow-up.
- Ask a few more questions about the hog data.

Assignment Choices

ACE questions 5, 10, 14, 15, and unassigned choices from earlier problems

Assessment

It is appropriate to use the check-up after this problem.

The table below gives data for the 15 North Carolina counties with the greatest 1993 hog populations. For each county, the table gives the 1993 hog population, the percent growth from 1983 to 1993, and the number of hogs per square mile.

County	1993 hog population	Growth from 1983	Hogs per square mile
Sampson	1,152,000	363%	1218
Duplin	1,041,000	349%	1273
Wayne	333,000	265%	603
Bladen	271,000	1178%	310
Greene	231,000	82%	870
Pitt	193,000	128%	297
Lenoir	159,000	312%	399
Johnston	129,000	61%	163
Robeson	124,000	81%	131
Onslow	115,000	261%	150
Jones	105,000	999%	223
Beaufort	103,000	51%	125
Pender	97,000	588%	111
Halifax	82,000	18%	113
Northampton	81,000	53%	151

Source: U.S. Department of Agriculture, as reported in the *Raleigh News and Observer,* 19–26 February 1995.

Problem 3.4

A. Write at least three statements comparing the hog data for Johnston County with the hog data for Bladen County.

B. Choose two different pairs of counties from the table. For each pair, write at least three statements comparing the hog data for the two counties.

Problem 3.4 Follow-Up

Find the mean and median of the 1993 hog populations for the 15 counties. How do the mean and median compare? If they are different, explain why. How do the mean and median help in describing the hog populations of these counties?

Answers to Problem 3.4

See page 37h.

Answer to Problem 3.4 Follow-Up

The mean is 281,067. The median is 129,000. The mean is greater because the top two population figures are far greater than the others; in fact, the population of hogs in the top two counties is greater than the combined populations of all the other counties. The mean tells us how many hogs would be in each county if we were to redistribute the hogs equally among the counties; the median tells us the middle population of the rank order if the counties are ordered by population.

Applications • Connections • Extensions

As you work on these ACE questions, use your calculator whenever you need it.

Applications

In 1–7, use the following table, which gives data regarding U.S. casualties in major wars from the Revolutionary War to the Persian Gulf War. A dash (—) indicates that the information is not available.

War	People serving	Battle deaths	Other deaths	Battle injuries	Total casualties
Revolutionary War	184,000 to 250,000	6824	18,500	8445	33,769
War of 1812	286,730	2260	—	4505	6765
Mexican War	78,718	1733	11,550	4152	17,435
Civil War (Union)	2,213,363	140,414	224,097	281,881	646,392
Civil War (Confederate)	600,000 to 1,500,000	74,524	59,297	—	133,821
Spanish-American War	306,760	385	2061	1662	4108
World War I	4,743,826	53,513	63,195	204,002	320,710
World War II	16,353,659	292,131	115,185	670,846	1,078,162
Korean War	5,764,143	33,651	—	103,284	136,939
Vietnam War	8,744,000	47,369	10,799	153,303	211,471
Persian Gulf War	467,539	148	145	467	760

Source: Revolutionary War: *The Toll of Independence,* Ed. Howard H. Peckham, Chicago: University of Chicago Press, 1974. All other wars: U.S. Department of Defense, as reported in *The World Almanac and Book of Facts 1996.* Ed. Robert Famighetti. Mahwah, New Jersey: Funk and Wagnalls, 1995.

1. In World War II, 16,353,659 Americans served in the fighting forces. Write this number in words.

2. In the Civil War, 2,213,363 people served in the Union army. Write this number in words.

3. Rank the ten wars from greatest to least in terms of the number of people serving. (Combine Union and Confederate data for the Civil War.)

Answers

Applications

1. sixteen million, three hundred fifty-three thousand, six hundred fifty-nine

2. two million, two hundred thirteen thousand, three hundred sixty-three

3. World War II, Vietnam War, Korean War, World War I, Civil War, Persian Gulf War, Spanish-American War, War of 1812, Revolutionary War, Mexican War (**Teaching Tip:** You might ask students how confident they are about the accuracy of these data and how the data from long ago might have been obtained.)

4. World War II, Civil War, World War I, Vietnam War, Korean War, Revolutionary War, Mexican War, War of 1812, Spanish-American War, Persian Gulf War

5a. See page 37h.

5b. Civil War and/or Mexican War, Revolutionary War, World War I, World War II, Korean War, Vietnam War and War of 1812, Spanish-American War, Persian Gulf War

5c. The rankings are different. The war with the greatest number serving (World War II, with 16,353,659) did have the greatest number of casualties (1,078,162) but not the greatest percent of casualties (6.6%); the Civil War had the greatest percent (21.0% to 27.7%). This is because circumstances in every war are different and people do not become casualties in the same ratio in every war.

6. See below right.

7. The five greatest numbers are all of the number of people serving: World War II, 16,400,000; Vietnam War, 8,700,000; Korean War, 5,800,000; World War I, 4,700,000; Civil War (Union), 2,200,000.

Connections

8. See page 37h.

9. See page 37h.

4. Rank the wars from greatest to least in terms of the total number of casualties. (Combine Union and Confederate data for the Civil War.)

5. a. For each war, what percent of the number of people serving were casualties? (Combine Union and Confederate data for the Civil War.)

b. Using the percents you found in part a, rank the wars from the greatest percent of casualties to the least percent of casualties.

c. How does this ranking compare with the rankings you made in questions 3 and 4? Give possible reasons for any differences in the rankings.

6. a. For each war, find the total number of deaths.

b. Round your answers from part a to the nearest thousand.

7. Find the five greatest numbers in the table, and round each to the nearest hundred thousand.

Connections

8. Suppose you play a two-digit version of Dialing Digits (from Problem 3.1).

a. What is the greatest number you could create?

b. What is the probability of getting this number on two spins?

c. If the result of the first spin is recorded in the first blank, what is the probability of getting a two-digit number in the forties?

9. Most of the war data used in questions 1–7 appear to be given as exact counts.

a. Which numbers do you think are probably most accurate?

b. If you wanted to round the data so you could make quick comparisons of size, what rounding would you use in each column? Why?

6.

War	a. Deaths	b. Rounded
Revolutionary War	25,324	25,000
War of 1812	at least 2260	at least 2000
Mexican War	13,283	13,000
Civil War	498,332	498,000
Spanish-American War	2446	2000
World War I	116,708	117,000
World War II	407,316	407,000
Korean War	at least 33,651	at least 34,000
Vietnam War	58,168	58,000
Persian Gulf War	293	0

10. To make sense of the war data used in questions 1–7, you may find it helpful to compare the numbers with more familiar data.

a. Find the three wars in which the greatest number of people served. Use the table on page 27 to find metropolitan areas and cities with populations approximately equal to the number of people serving in these wars.

b. Armies are usually made up of young people. Find out the number of students in the senior class of your community high school. Then, find the number of senior classes of that size needed to equal the 8,744,000 people who served in the Vietnam War.

11. A news report about lottery winnings stated, "Saturday's $43 million Lotto Jackpot equals a trail of $1 bills that would stretch 4100 miles, from New York City to San Francisco and back to Glacier National Park in Montana."

a. A $1 bill is about 6 inches long. How many $1 bills are needed to make a trail 1 mile long?

b. How many $1 bills are needed to make a trail 4100 miles long?

12. Look at the "Other deaths" column in the table of war data for questions 1–7.

a. What might cause "other deaths" during a war?

b. What might explain the changing proportion of "other deaths" to "battle deaths" from the Revolutionary War through the Persian Gulf War?

10a. The number who served in World War II, about 16 million, is about midway between the metropolitan-area populations of New York City and Los Angeles. The number who served in the Vietnam War, about 8,700,000, is a bit greater than the population of metropolitan Chicago. The number who served in the Korean War, about 5,800,000, is close to the population of metropolitan Philadelphia.

10b. Answers will vary. For a senior class of about 250 students, $8,744,000 \div 250 \approx 35,000$ senior classes would be needed to equal the number of people who served in Vietnam.

11a. 1 mile = 5280 feet, and each foot will have 2 bills, so $5280 \times 2 = 10,560$ bills

11b. $4100 \times 10,560 = 43,296,000$ bills

12a. Possible answer: Other deaths might be caused by accidents and illness.

12b. Possible answer: In earlier wars, the number of other deaths is greater than the number of battle deaths. Improved medical treatments, medicines (including antibiotics), and sanitation have probably had a great impact on reducing the number of war deaths from other causes.

13a. *greatest population:* China, 1,070,000,000; *least population:* Israel, 4,000,000

13b. *greatest military:* Soviet Union, 4,400,000; *least military:* Israel, 180,000

13c. *greatest percent in military:* Iraq, 900,000 ÷ 17,000,000 ≈ 0.053, or about 5.3%; *least percent in military:* India, 1,502,000 ÷ 790,000,000 ≈ 0.002, or about 0.2%

13. This table shows 1987 data for ten countries. For each country, the table gives the number of people serving in the military and the total population. Notice that the numbers of people in the military are given in thousands. For example, the number of people in the military in China is $3530 \times 1000 = 3{,}530{,}000$. The populations are given in millions. For example, the population of China is $1070 \times 1{,}000{,}000 = 1{,}070{,}000{,}000$.

Country	Number in military (thousands)	Population (millions)
People's Republic of China	3530	1070
Cuba	297	10
India	1502	790
Iraq	900	17
Israel	180	4
North Korea	838	21
Soviet Union	4400	284
Syria	400	11
United States	2279	245
Vietnam	1300	64

Source: *The World Almanac and Book of Facts 1992.* New York: Pharos Books, 1991.

a. Which of the countries listed have the greatest and least populations, and what are those populations? Write your answers in *standard notation.* That is, show all the places of each number. For example, the population of Cuba in standard notation is 10,000,000.

b. Which of the countries listed have the largest and smallest military forces, and what are the sizes of those military forces? Write your answers in standard notation.

c. Which of the countries listed have the greatest and least percents of their population serving in the military, and what are those percents?

14. In Problem 3.4, you looked at the 15 North Carolina counties with the largest 1993 hog populations. The bar graph below compares the total hog population of these counties with the total human population of these counties for every even year from 1984 through 1994. How do you think the 1995 hog population compared with the 1995 human population?

Hog Boom

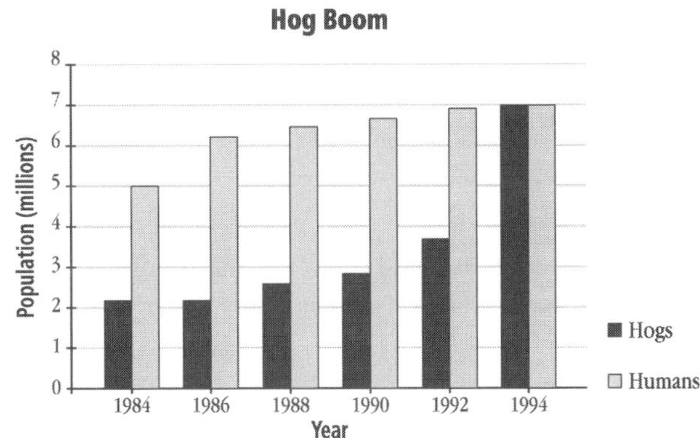

15. The table below shows the change in the "hog inventory" from 1993 to 1994 for the five North Carolina counties with the highest 1994 hog populations.

a. If the percent change for each county was the same from 1994 to 1995 as it was from 1993 to 1994, how many hogs were in each county in 1995?

b. Use the information in the table to figure out what the hog inventory for Bladen County was in 1993. How does this number compare with the total 1993 hog population of Bladen County given in the table in Problem 3.4?

County	1994 hog inventory (millions)	Growth from 1993
Duplin	1.47	41%
Sampson	1.45	26%
Wayne	0.41	23%
Bladen	0.41	50%
Greene	0.28	22%

Note: The hog inventory is the number of hogs and pigs on farms as of December 1, 1994.
Source: North Carolina Department of Agriculture.

14. The hog population is growing much faster than the human population, so it probably surpassed the human population in 1995.

15a. Duplin, 2.07 million; Sampson, 1.83 million; Wayne, 0.50 million; Bladen, 0.62 million; Greene, 0.34 million

15b. The number of hogs in 1994 in Bladen County, 410,000, is 1.5 times the number in 1993; therefore, the number in 1993 is 410,000 ÷ 1.5 = 273,333, or about 273,000 hogs. The total given in the table for Problem 3.4 is 271,000, which is a bit less. The difference might be due to rounding or to the different sources of the data.

Extensions

16. from 105 miles up to, but not including, 115 miles

17. from 122,500 feet up to, but not including, 127,500 feet

18. from 45 million up to, but not including, 55 million

19. from 115,000,000 up to, but not including, 125,000,000

Extensions

In 16–19, a number in the given statement has been rounded from its actual value. Give the greatest and least possible actual values for the number.

16. The longest traffic jam of all time was 110 miles long (rounded to the nearest 10 miles).

17. The longest bridge in the United States is the Second Lake Pontchartrain Causeway in Louisiana. It is 125,000 feet long (rounded to the nearest 5000 feet).

18. In 1991, there were 50 million (rounded to the nearest 10 million) pet dogs in the United States.

19. As of 1989, the United States had the greatest number of telephones of any country in the world, 120,000,000 (rounded to the nearest 10,000,000).

Mathematical Reflections

In this investigation, you compared, ordered, and rounded large numbers. These questions will help you summarize what you have learned:

1. Describe several ways you can compare large numbers. Be sure to discuss percents, differences, and ordering.
2. Tokyo-Yokohama, Japan, is the most populous city in the world with 28,477,000 residents (as of 1995). How would you round this population to the nearest ten million? To the nearest million? To the nearest hundred thousand? Choose one of these three roundings, and describe a situation in which it would make sense to use this rounding. Explain your reasoning.
3. Describe some ways you could compare the population of Tokyo-Yokohama with the population of the largest metropolitan area in the United States.

Think about your answers to these questions, discuss your ideas with other students and your teacher, and then write a summary of your findings in your journal.

Possible Answers

1. You can compare a set of large numbers by ordering them from least to greatest or vice versa. You can find the difference between numbers to show how much greater one number is than another. If information is given about the rate of growth, the percent growth can be computed. This growth can be used to compare amounts.

2. This number can be rounded to 30,000,000; 28,000,000; and 28,500,000. It would make sense to use the rounding to the nearest 10 million, 30,000,000, if you were comparing the population of this city with the population of the world, which could be similarly rounded.

3. The largest metropolitan area in the United States is the New York City area, at 19,549,649 (in 1992). The population of Tokyo exceeds the population of New York by about 8,927,000 people. Also, Tokyo's population is about 1.46 times the population of New York. You could also compare the densities—people per square mile or square kilometer—if you knew the land areas of each city.

Tips for the Linguistically Diverse Classroom

Original Rebus The Original Rebus technique is described in detail in *Getting to Know Connected Mathematics*. Students make a copy of the text before it is discussed. During the discussion, they generate their own rebuses for words they do not understand; the words are made comprehensible through pictures, objects, or demonstrations. Example: Question 1—Key phrases for which students might make rebuses are *compare* (>, <), *large numbers* (X00,000,000,000), *percents* (%), *differences* (–), *ordering* (1, 2, 3).

3.1 • Playing Dialing Digits

In this problem, students play a spinner game that combines random variation with strategy based on an understanding of place value and probability. In the process, they review our place-value system and the reading of large numbers.

Launch

To introduce the investigation, you might write the number 4,961,529,000,000 on the board, which is the estimated 1995 national debt of the U.S. government in dollars, and ask:

How would you read this number?

To avoid having one student answer the question for the whole class, you might ask students to consult in pairs about how the number should be read before they share their ideas.

If it seems necessary to review the place value of each period (ones, thousands, millions, billions, trillions), point out to students that if they can read numbers through hundreds, all they must do to read larger numbers is to attach the correct period names.

For the Teacher: More Practice in Reading Large Numbers

If students need more practice, it may be interesting to offer them earlier figures describing the U.S. national debt.

Year	National Debt
1945	$260,123,000,000
1955	$274,366,000,000
1965	$322,318,000,000
1975	$541,925,000,000
1985	$1,817,521,000,000
1995	$4,961,529,000,000

On October 29, 1996, the debt was $5,229,978,532,589 and was increasing by an average of $659 million per day. The current debt is available on the U.S. National Debt Clock on the World Wide Web.

Next, raise the more fundamental question of how one can comprehend the magnitude of such a number.

What does it mean to be $5,229,978,532,589 in debt? How can we think about this large amount?

The population of the United States is about 260,000,000. *(Write this number on the board.)* If the debt were shared equally among all the people in the United States, how much would each person's share be? *(about $19,100)*

For the Teacher: Working with Large Numbers on a Calculator

Students' calculators may not be able to accept so many digits. You may want to talk with them about doing calculations like these by using tricks such as truncating zeros. However, it is very important that they understand what they are doing and why it works, not just perform the operation to arrive at an answer.

Many non–graphing calculators will accept only eight-digit numbers, meaning that the numbers involved in the problem above—260,000,000 and 4,961,529,000,000—cannot be entered. To be able to operate with these numbers with the aid of a calculator, one can enter truncated forms of the numbers; for example, 260 and 4,961,529. The same number of zeros has been removed from each number. Another way to approach this problem is to think of 260,000,000 as 260 million and of 4,961,529,000,000 as 4,961,529 million.

After performing an operation with truncated numbers, many students find it difficult to interpret what number their answer represents. For example, when truncating the same number of zeros from each number, these ideas must be understood:

- If you add or subtract the numbers, you will need to add to the answer the same number of zeros that were truncated.
- If you multiply the numbers, you will need to add a greater number of zeros to the result.
- If you divide the numbers, you obtain the same result you would have had you used the original numbers.

It is not recommended teaching traditional rules at this point but instead focusing on the relationships among standard notation, truncated numbers, and arithmetic operations. Investigating simpler problems, in which students know the answers intuitively, can help students to develop their own rules. For example, students could add, subtract, multiply, and divide such pairs of numbers as 7000 and 500; 12,000 and 2000; and 40,000 and 800; looking for patterns in the answers. Using this technique to help students to develop their own rules puts to use the powerful problem-solving strategy "make a simpler problem."

Introduce the Dialing Digits game. The rules for the game are outlined in the student edition, but the best way to get students started is to demonstrate a couple of spins using the spinner on Transparency 3.1A. Place the point of a pen or pencil through the rounded end of a bobby pin or paper clip and on the center of the spinner. Flick the bobby pin with your finger. Let the class decide where they would put each resulting number.

After students have a sense of the game, have them play against another students, or put students in pairs and have teams of two play against each other. Distribute a copy of the spinner from Labsheet 3.1A, a paper clip, and game cards from Labsheet 3.1B to each player or team.

Explore

Students should play the game several times, rotating to compete with a different player or team for each game.

As you observe students playing, try to verify that all team members are involved in deciding where to place each digit. If necessary, remind teams to keep their numbers hidden from the other team. If any team complains about their opponents taking too long to make a decision, encourage them to reach an agreement among themselves about how many seconds will be allowed for placing each digit.

The problem asks students to write down any winning strategies they discover. Encourage students to discuss strategies for where to place each number.

The follow-up poses two variations of the game. Save these for after the summary.

Summarize

Let students share the strategies they found. There is no certain winning strategy, but students' strategies will likely involve some version of the idea of placing greater numbers farther to the left, which emphasizes the connection of the game to the concept of place value.

When playing Dialing Digits, players will often find themselves wondering how long to wait for a number to place in the position with the greatest place value. This is a good opportunity to raise a few questions about probability with the class.

> What is the probability of getting an 8 or 9 on a spin? *(Each of the ten possible digits has the same probability of being spun, so there is a probability of $0.1 + 0.1 = 0.2$, or $\frac{2}{10}$, of getting an 8 or 9.)*
>
> What is the greatest number you can make from the nine digits that were spun in your last game? What is the least number you could make from those digits?
>
> For each game, you spun the spinner nine times. How many different ways can the nine numbers that you spun in your last game be arranged in the spaces? *(If all of the numbers are different, there are $9 \times 8 \times 7 \times 6 \times 5 \times 4 \times 3 \times 2 \times 1$ possible arrangements. If some numbers are the same, there are fewer arrangements.)*

Have the class play one of the variations of Dialing Digits that are described in the follow-up. Determining a winner by the sum of two rounds of the game or by the difference between two rounds of the game adds intriguing twists to the strategies students will discover. In the sum game, each number should be as great as possible. In the difference game, the first-round number should be the greatest possible and the second-round number should be the least possible. Students may ask whether they can put a zero in the first digit's place. The class or you will have to make a decision about this. You could let the class play the game and deal with this issue when it arises.

Once students have explored one of the variations of the game, ask:

> What is the greatest possible sum (difference) in this new game?

Reading large numbers is a minor aspect of Dialing Digits, but the game is an enjoyable way to sharpen number-reading skills. You may want to create a new game board with more places, including some to the right of the decimal point, and have students play the game again.

3.2 • Getting Things in Order

This problem is a review as well as an extension of the ideas about ordering numbers that students have developed in earlier grades. The study of the population data also has interesting connections to the field of geography.

Launch

Describe what is meant by the term *metropolitan area.* For example, the Phoenix metropolitan area includes the cities of Phoenix, Mesa, Tempe, and other surrounding suburbs.

Read through the problem with the class. Have students work in groups of two or three on the questions, but ask each student to keep a record of the answers.

Explore

If students struggle with part B, ask how they might compare two metropolitan areas such as Atlanta and Washington, D.C. Then, ask them to generalize how they compared these two areas.

In part C, students locate the metropolitan areas on the map on Labsheet 3.2. They may need reference books or maps to do this part of the problem.

As students finish the problem, have them move on to the follow-up.

Summarize

Ask for the ranking of the 20 metropolitan areas from most populated to least populated, and list the areas on the board or add ranks to the list on Transparency 3.2A.

> How did you rank the metropolitan areas?

Some students will say that they looked for the populations that had the most digits. Los Angeles and New York both have eight digits in their population figures, which means they both have 10 million or more residents. Between these two cities, you have only to find the one with the greatest number of millions (New York, with 19). The remaining cities can be ordered by the number of millions. For those with the same number of millions (such as Atlanta and Cleveland, with 2 million), you can compare the next place value, hundred thousands.

Display a transparency of Labsheet 3.2, a U.S. map, or Transparency 3.2C, and have the class locate each metropolitan area. (Transparency 3.2C is the same map shown on Labsheet 3.2 but with the areas located.) Place the rank of each area in the appropriate location.

Why might large metropolitan areas be located where they are?

Discuss reasons for the population differences of these metropolitan areas. Some students may be curious about which areas are increasing or decreasing in population and in the rate of change. This kind of information can be found in almanacs and similar resources.

Talk about the questions raised in part C.

How might the locations of these areas affect the decisions that governments and businesses must make?

In the discussion of this question, make sure these points are raised:

- Coastal areas and rivers are places that were settled first, and they are still viable outlets for trade with other cities and countries.
- Mountain and desert areas tend to discourage large settlements because they do not have good farmland and are not as easy to live in.

You may want to talk with the social studies teachers about how this lesson might be connected with work being done in other classes.

In the follow-up, students will have discovered that the ordering of the major cities is quite different from the ordering of the related metropolitan areas. Ask them what factors might cause these differences.

3.3 • Rounding Numbers

This problem will engage students in thinking about appropriate degrees of accuracy in rounding large numbers. As the student edition points out, it is often easier to work with approximate values for large numbers. It is common for data in tables to be written as truncated values with a phrase such as "in thousands" or "in millions" in the table heading.

Launch

Read through the problem introduction, and discuss the examples about the rounding of the population of Los Angeles. Have students explain why each number is rounded as it is. This should be a review for most students.

The problem is not asking students to round numbers but rather to make sense of rounded numbers and to choose an appropriate rounding scheme for comparing two pieces of data. This will be a new idea for most students. You might want to give students the problem and see what sense they make of it, and address any misconceptions during the summary. Or, discuss one of the three parts of the problem as a class, and then have students work with a partner on the other two parts and the follow-up, which does ask them to do some rounding of numbers.

Have students work in pairs on the problem and follow-up.

Explore

If students are struggling with the problem, suggest that they do the follow-up first, which will give them more practice with rounding.

When pairs work on the follow-up, monitor the discussion for interesting and reasonable decisions about how to round the population figures. Students may have reasons for why more than one estimate is appropriate for a particular figure, depending on how the rounded number will be used. Be sure to call on pairs that have good ideas during the summary.

Summarize

Allow time for several pairs to share their answers and to discuss how they reasoned about the problem.

In part A, the world population is rounded to the nearest hundred million (5.7 billion). Therefore, it is reasonable to use 200,000,000, which is also rounded to the nearest hundred million, when comparing the two populations. If students don't bring up this idea of common place-value rounding, add the idea to the conversation yourself.

Talk about the follow-up, which asks students to round the population figures of the 20 metropolitan areas.

> How did you round the numbers? Why did you decide to round them that way?

Students might suggest rounding to the nearest ten thousand so that each area will retain the same rank. Rounding to any higher place value will change the order of the areas. While there are formal rules for this procedure, and those rules are often drilled at great length, common sense is the best guideline.

3.4 • Comparing Hog Populations

In this problem, students compare hog populations in counties in North Carolina over a ten-year interval, comparing the actual numbers of hogs, hogs per square mile, and the percent change in the population over the period.

Launch

Talk about the story related in the "Did you know?" feature about the Onslow County hog-waste disaster. Then ask:

> What industries in our area might affect the quality of the air or water?

> Who might be interested in information about the populations of hogs in North Carolina?

The data might be of interest to a local business that sells food for hogs. A business that manufactures food for hogs and is considering locating in North Carolina may be interested in the hog-population growth in the various counties. Someone monitoring the potential harm caused by hog farms or a local developer may be interested in the hogs-per-square-mile data.

Display Transparency 3.4, if possible, which contains the table of hog-population data.

> How might you compare the hog data for the various counties listed here?

When a few ideas have been proposed, have students work in pairs on the problem and follow-up.

Explore

As pairs work, check the kinds of statements they are writing. If all the comparisons they are making are of the same type, such as stating differences, ask them to make another kind of comparison.

Summarize

Have pairs get together in groups of four to share their comparisons. Each pair will read their comparisons as the other pair listens, questioning anything that doesn't make sense. Then, have each foursome share one of their comparisons with the class for discussion.

In the follow-up, pairs look at the mean and median as other methods of interpreting data. Discuss students' solutions and how they arrived at their answers. This will review these concepts for students who have forgotten or who need another opportunity to work with statistical measures.

Once the problem and the follow-up have been summarized, ask a few more questions about the data.

> To what degree of accuracy do you think these numbers were reported?
>
> How do you think the rates of growth were determined?
>
> What would it mean if the number of seventh graders in our school grew by 300%? If our seventh grade class has a population of ______, what would the population be if it grew by 300%?
>
> Why might it be important to look at population growth rates?
>
> What was the population of hogs in Sampson and Bladen Counties in 1983? How did you find that number? Did anyone do the problem in a different way?
>
> If the present rate of growth is maintained, what will the hog populations of Sampson and Bladen Counties be in 2003? How did you find that number? Did anyone do the problem in a different way?

Additional Answers

Answers to Problem 3.4

A. Possible answer: The hog population of Bladen County was more than twice the hog population of Johnston County in 1993, but this was not true in 1983. The rate of growth between 1983 and 1993 in the hog population of Bladen County is more than 19 times what it is for Johnston County. Bladen County has almost twice the number of hogs per square mile as does Johnston County.

B. Answers will vary. Possible answer: Robeson County has 42,000 more hogs than does Halifax County. The number of hogs in Robeson County is a little more than half again the number in Halifax County, yet the number of hogs per square mile is close—131 in Robeson compared to 113 in Halifax. Robeson's hog population has grown at four times the rate Halifax's population has grown.

ACE Answers

Applications

5a.

War	Percent of those serving who were casualties
Revolutionary War	13.5% to 18.4%
War of 1812	at least 2.4%
Mexican War	22.1%
Civil War	21.0% to 27.7%
Spanish-American War	1.3%
World War I	6.8%
World War II	6.6%
Korean War	at least 2.4%
Vietnam War	2.4%
Persian Gulf War	0.16%

Connections

8a. 99

8b. There is a $\frac{1}{10}$ probability of getting 9 on the first spin and a $\frac{1}{10}$ probability of getting 9 on the second spin, so the probability of getting 99 is $\frac{1}{100}$.

8c. Getting a number in the forties means that you spin a 4 on the first spin. This has a probability of occurring of $\frac{1}{10}$.

9a. Possible answer: The more recent data are most likely to be accurate. Of those figures, the numbers of deaths are most likely to be accurate. (**Teaching Tip:** You might point out that we often can't determine exact numbers for things we want to measure.)

9b. Possible answer: Rounding to one or two significant figures probably makes the most sense. For example, the number serving in the Vietnam War can be rounded to 8,700,000, while the battle deaths in the Mexican War can be rounded to 1700. Or, one could round each column to the greatest place value of the smallest value in the column. If the numbers are too close and this rounding distorts the facts, you could round to a lesser place value. For example, you could round each entry in the "People serving" column to the nearest ten thousand and maintain enough accuracy to compare the numbers in that column.

INVESTIGATION 4

How Many Is a Million?

Practical number sense encompasses the ability to deal with large numbers. To be able to reason about or interpret realistic information involving large numbers, quantities in millions, billions, and trillions must make some sense. It is also important to be able to interpret number names in writing and orally and to express large numbers using standard and scientific notation.

In Problem 4.1, Thinking Big, students make sense of a million by answering questions such as "How long does it take your heart to beat 1,000,000 times?" and "How many students can stand inside a square with an area of 1,000,000 square centimeters?" In Problem 4.2, Thinking Even Bigger, students imagine and work with collections of unit cubes to make sense of a million, a billion, and a trillion. Their work leads naturally into writing numbers in scientific notation. Problem 4.3, Using Scientific Notation, introduces students to scientific and calculator notation for large numbers.

Mathematical and Problem-Solving Goals

- *To build a concrete understanding of a million in a variety of contexts*
- *To review and extend the concept of place value as it relates to reading, writing, and using large numbers*
- *To review and extend the use of exponents*
- *To write and interpret large numbers using scientific and calculator notation*
- *To estimate with large numbers*

Materials

Problem	For students	For the teacher
All	Graphing calculators	Transparencies 4.1 to 4.3 (optional)
4.1	Metersticks (1 per group)	
4.2	Labsheet 4.2 (optional), sets of base ten blocks (optional), unit cubes (as many as you have available)	Transparency of Labsheet 4.2 (optional)
4.3		Overhead graphing calculator (optional)

Student Pages 38–50 Teaching the Investigation 50a–50g

Thinking Big

At a Glance

Grouping: groups of 3 or 4

Launch

- Begin a discussion about the meaning of one million.
- Encourage the class to bring in examples of the use of millions, billions, and trillions.
- Ask students to make a prediction for each situation in the problem and to talk about what they might do to answer each question.
- Have groups work on the problem and follow-up.

Explore

- If groups want to divide the work among their members, remind them that they must all agree on the answers.

Summarize

- Have groups share their answers and reasoning for each part of the problem.
- Ask students to read their questions for the follow-up.

How Many Is a Million?

You have seen that it is sometimes difficult to get a sense of just how big a large number really is. In previous investigations, you developed some benchmarks to help you imagine large numbers. In this investigation, you will develop a sense of how many a million is. You will also learn a shorthand notation for writing large numbers.

4.1 Thinking Big

Large numbers appear in newspaper, radio, and television reports every day.

The Daily Gazette

VOL. CXXXIV NO. 24 FRIDAY, MAY 23, 1997 ★★★★

Hog Lagoon Spills a Million Gallons of Waste in Creek!

Fish Kill Expected to Run into Millions!

How many is a million? This problem will give you a sense of what a million "looks like."

Problem 4.1

For each part of this problem, explain how you arrived at your answer.

A. How long does it take your heart to beat 1,000,000 times?

B. Advertisements for a popular brand of chocolate chip cookie claim that there are 1000 chips in each bag of cookies. How many bags would you need to have 1,000,000 chips? If one bag measures 20 centimeters by 12 centimeters by 6 centimeters, would all of these bags fit in your classroom?

C. If someone is 1,000,000 hours old, what is his or her age in years?

D. How many students can stand inside a square with an area of 1,000,000 square centimeters?

Assignment Choices

ACE questions 1–3 and unassigned choices from earlier problems

Answers to Problem 4.1

A. Possible answer: A heart that beats 70 times in one minute will beat $70 \times 60 = 4200$ times in one hour and $4200 \times 24 = 100{,}800$ times in one day. Thus it would take $1{,}000{,}000 \div 100{,}800 \approx 9.9$ days for the number of heartbeats to reach 1,000,000.

B. You would need 1000 bags to get 1,000,000 chips. The volume of 1000 bags is $20 \times 12 \times 6 \times 1000 = 1{,}440{,}000$ cm^3, or 1.44 m^3, which will fit into any classroom.

C. As 1,000,000 hours $\div$ 24 = 41,667 days, and assuming 365 days in a year, this person is $41{,}667 \div 365 \approx 114$ years old.

D. Possible answer: We could get 7 students in a square measuring 100 cm by 100 cm, or 10,000 cm^2. As $1{,}000{,}000 \div 10{,}000 = 100$, 100 squares of this size would fit in a square with an area of 1,000,000 cm^2. So, about $7 \times 100 = 700$ students could stand in the larger square.

Problem 4.1 Follow-Up

Write another question you could ask to help someone get a sense of how many a million is.

4.2 Thinking Even Bigger

The questions in Problem 4.1 helped you get a sense of how many a million is. But what about a billion or a trillion? How can you make sense of newspaper headlines like these?

The Daily Gazette

VOL. CXXI NO. 7 | THURSDAY, OCTOBER 2, 1995 | ★★★★

U.S. Debt Nears $5 Trillion

Population of India Passes 1 Billion

Did you know?

The words *billion* and *trillion* do not mean the same thing in Great Britain as they do in the United States. In the United States, when we say "a million," "a billion," and "a trillion," we mean these numbers:

1 million = 1,000,000
1 billion = 1,000,000,000
1 trillion = 1,000,000,000,000

In Great Britain, a million is 1,000,000, as it is in the United States, but a billion is 1,000,000,000,000—the number we call a trillion. And a trillion is 1,000,000,000,000,000,000.

Thinking Even Bigger

At a Glance

***Grouping:* groups of 2 or 3**

Launch

- Discuss the introduction to the problem.
- Talk about things involving millions, billions, and trillions.
- Have students work in groups of two or three on the problem and follow-up.

Explore

- Encourage students to build models or make sketches of the arrangements.

Summarize

- Ask students to share how they found the number of cubes in each arrangement.
- Help the class summarize what they know about place value, perhaps using the chart on Transparency 4.2B.

Answer to Problem 4.1 Follow-Up

Possible answers: If the average teenager spends 13 hours a week watching television, how many teenagers need to watch television in one day to make a total viewing time of 1,000,000 minutes? How many minutes does it take to dribble a basketball 1,000,000 times?

Assignment Choices

ACE questions 4, 5, 11–13, 17, 20, and unassigned choices from earlier problems (It is important to assign 11–13, as the review of factorization and exponents will help students use scientific notation in Problem 4.3.)

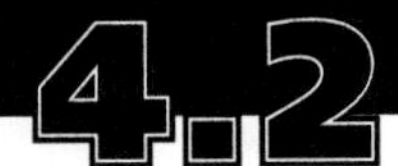

In this problem, you will try to imagine a million, a billion, and a trillion as collections of unit cubes. To start, you can line up ten unit cubes to form a *long*. You can then put ten longs together to make a *flat*.

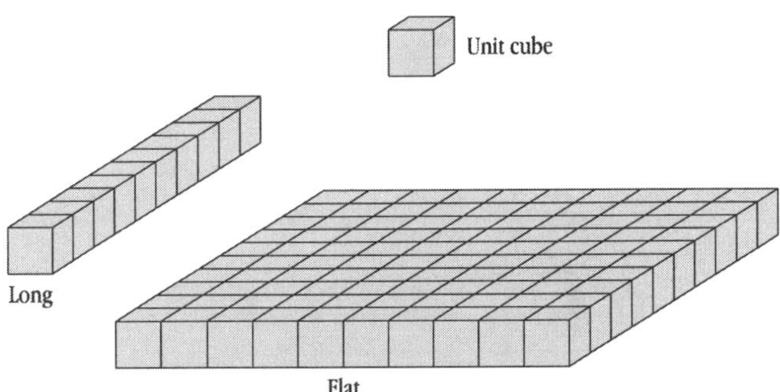

Problem 4.2

A. How many unit cubes are needed to make one *flat*?

B. You can stack ten flats to make a ***super cube***. How many unit cubes are needed to make a super cube?

C. You can line up ten super cubes to make a ***super long***. How many unit cubes are needed to make a super long?

D. You can put together ten super longs to make a ***super flat***. How many unit cubes are needed to make a super flat?

E. You can put together ten super flats to make a ***super-duper cube***. How many unit cubes are needed to make a super-duper cube?

Problem 4.2 Follow-Up

1. How many unit cubes would it take to build a *super-duper long* (made of ten super-duper cubes)? What are the dimensions of a super-duper long?
2. How many unit cubes would it take to build a *super-duper flat* (made of ten super-duper longs)? What are the dimensions of a super-duper flat?
3. How many unit cubes would it take to build an *extra-super-duper cube* (made of ten super-duper flats)? What are the dimensions of an extra-super-duper cube?
4. Which of the super, super-duper, or extra-super-duper arrangements contain more than a million unit cubes? More than a billion unit cubes? More than a trillion unit cubes?

Answers to Problem 4.2

A. 100 B. 1000 C. 10,000 D. 100,000

E. 1,000,000 (This is 1000 super cubes.)

Answers to Problem 4.2 Follow-Up

1. 10,000,000 cubes; $1000 \times 100 \times 100$
2. 100,000,000 cubes; $1000 \times 1000 \times 100$
3. 1,000,000,000 cubes; $1000 \times 1000 \times 1000$
4. The super-duper long, the super-duper flat, and the extra-super-duper cube all have more than a million cubes. None of the figures has more than a billion cubes, though the extra-super-duper cube has exactly a billion cubes. None of the figures has a trillion cubes.

4.3 Using Scientific Notation

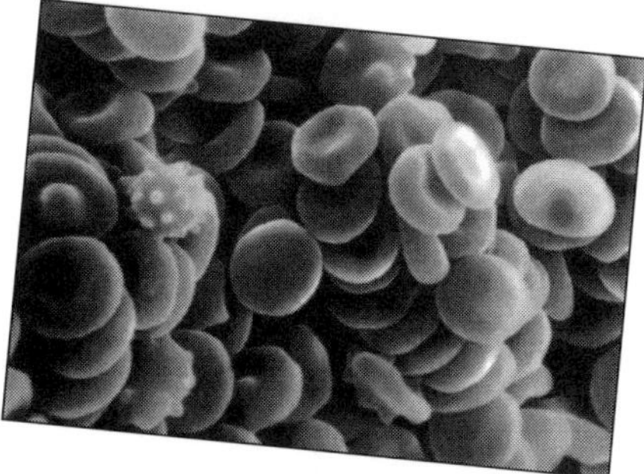

Numbers used in scientific work are often very large. For example, there are about 33,400,000,000,000,000,000,000 molecules in 1 gram of water. There are about 25,000,000,000,000 red blood cells in a human body. According to the big bang theory in astronomy, our universe began with an explosion 18,000,000,000 years ago, generating temperatures of 100,000,000,000° Celsius.

A calculator is a useful tool for working with large numbers. However, to use your calculator effectively, you need to understand the special way it handles large numbers.

Think about this!

- Try entering 25,000,000,000,000 on your calculator. Does your calculator allow you to enter all the digits? If you are using a graphing calculator, press [ENTER] after you enter the number. What do you think the resulting display means?
- Use your calculator to find 500,000 × 500,000. What do you think the resulting display means?
- What does the [^] or [y^x] key tell your calculator to do?
- Enter 10 [^] 5, 10 [^] 8, and 10 [^] 12 on your calculator (if you are using a nongraphing calculator, you will need to press 10 [y^x] 5, 10 [y^x] 8, and 10 [y^x] 12). What do you think the resulting displays mean?

The product of 500,000 × 500,000 is 250,000,000,000. However, when you tried to compute this product on your calculator, the display probably showed one of these results:

`2.5E11` or `2.5   11`

Your calculator did not make a mistake. It was using a special notation.

4.3 Using Scientific Notation

At a Glance

Grouping: pairs

Launch

- Have students explore the examples in the "Think about this!" feature and discuss their results.
- Talk about the different types of notation.

Explore

- Encourage students to share what they know about working with calculators.
- Help students who have trouble with part E.
- Save the follow-up for the summary.

Summarize

- Discuss the answers to the problem.
- Have students work on the follow-up individually and share answers in pairs.
- If students still need practice, offer a few more problems.

Assignment Choices

ACE questions 6–10, 14–16, 18, 19, and unassigned choices from earlier problems

To understand your calculator's notation, let's start by looking at a short way to write 100,000,000,000:

$$100{,}000{,}000{,}000 = 10 \times 10 \times 10 \times 10 \times 10 \times 10 \times 10 \times 10 \times 10 \times 10 \times 10$$
$$= 10^{11}$$

In the notation 10^{11}, 10 is the ***base*** and 11 is the ***exponent***. The exponent tells you how many times the base is used as a factor.

We can use this short way of writing 100,000,000,000 to find a short way to write 250,000,000,000:

$$250{,}000{,}000{,}000 = 2.5 \times 100{,}000{,}000{,}000$$
$$= 2.5 \times 10^{11}$$

The number 2.5×10^{11} is written in scientific notation. A number is written in **scientific notation** if it is expressed in the following form:

a number greater than or equal to 1, but less than 10 × 10 raised to an exponent

Scientific notation looks a little different on a calculator. Your calculator was using scientific notation when it displayed

`2.5E11` or `2.5    11`

Both of these displays mean 2.5×10^{11}.

This example shows how you would use scientific notation to write 4,000,000:

$$4{,}000{,}000 = 4.0 \times 1{,}000{,}000$$
$$= 4.0 \times 10 \times 10 \times 10 \times 10 \times 10 \times 10$$
$$= 4.0 \times 10^{6}$$

How would your calculator display this number?

Answers to Problem 4.3

A. 1. 10,000,000,000,000,000,000,000
   2. 10,000,000,000,000
   3. 100,000,000,000
   4. 10,000,000,000

B. 1. 10^{12}
   2. 10^{6}

C. 1. 3,000,000,000
   2. 25,000,000,000,000
   3. 17,500,000,000

D. 1. 5×10^{6}
   2. 1.8×10^{7}
   3. 1.79×10^{10}

E. 1. 1,700,000,000,000; 1.7×10^{12}
   2. 1,700,000,000,000,000; 1.7×10^{15}
   3. 2,350,000,000,000; 2.35×10^{12}
   4. 36,980,000,000,000,000; 3.698×10^{16}

Problem 4.3

A. Write each number in standard notation.

1. 10^{22} **2.** 10^{13} **3.** 10^{11} **4.** 10^{10}

B. Write each number in a shorter form by using an exponent.

1. $10 \times 10 \times 10 \times 10 \times 10 \times 10 \times 10 \times 10 \times 10 \times 10 \times 10 \times 10$

2. 1,000,000

C. Write each number in standard notation.

1. 3.0×10^9 **2.** 2.5×10^{13} **3.** 1.75×10^{10}

D. Write each number in scientific notation.

1. 5,000,000 **2.** 18,000,000 **3.** 17,900,000,000

E. Experiment with your calculator to figure out how to get these displays. Then, write each number in both scientific and standard notation.

1. `1.7E12` or `1.7  12`

2. `1.7E15` or `1.7  15`

3. `2.35E12` or `2.35  12`

4. `3.698E16` or `3.698  16`

Problem 4.3 Follow-Up

1. Look back at your answers for parts C and D of Problem 4.3. Compare the scientific notation for each number with the standard notation. What connections do you see between the two notations?

2. Write each of the following as a product of the base, without using an exponent.

a. 10^4 **b.** 10^7 **c.** 7^3

3. Describe how you would translate a number written in scientific notation, such as 4×10^{13} or 3.5×10^7, into standard notation.

4. Describe how you would translate a number written in standard notation, such as 32,000,000, into scientific notation.

5. Write 45,671,234,142 in scientific notation.

Answers to Problem 4.3 Follow-Up

1. Possible answer: The expression 10^6 means multiply by six factors of 10, which is also written as 1,000,000. So, 5×10^6 means $5 \times 1{,}000{,}000$ or 5,000,000.
2. a. $10 \times 10 \times 10 \times 10$

   b. $10 \times 10 \times 10 \times 10 \times 10 \times 10 \times 10$

   c. $7 \times 7 \times 7$
3. See page 50g.
4. See page 50g.
5. $4.5671234142 \times 10^{10}$, which can be rounded to 4.57×10^{10}

Applications • Connections • Extensions

As you work on these ACE questions, use your calculator whenever you need it.

Applications

1. a. Is it possible for someone to be 1,000,000 minutes old? Explain.
   b. Is it possible for someone to be 1,000,000,000 minutes old? Explain.
2. How old would someone be if they were born 1,000,000 days ago?
3. A typical human heart beats about 70 times a minute.
   a. How long does it take a heart to beat 1,000,000 times?
   b. How long does it take a heart to beat 1,000,000,000 times?
   c. How can you use your answers from parts a and b to figure out how long it takes a heart to beat 1000 times or 1,000,000,000,000 times?
4. a. How many times a million is a billion?

   b. How many times a million is a trillion?
   c. How many times a billion is a trillion?
5. The diameter of a penny is about 2 centimeters.
   a. How many pennies, laid side by side, would you need to make a line 1000 kilometers long? (Recall that 1 kilometer = 1000 meters and 1 meter = 100 centimeters.)
   b. The distance across the United States at its widest point is 3000 miles. How many pennies, laid side by side, would you need to span this distance? (Recall that 1 mile ≈ 1.6 kilometers.)
6. The population of the world is about 5,700,000,000. Write this number in scientific notation.

Answers

Applications

1a. yes; A person who is 1,000,000 minutes old is about 1.9 years old: 1,000,000 minutes ÷ 60 minutes/hour ≈ 16,667 hours; 16,667 hours ÷ 24 hours/day ≈ 694 days; and 694 days ÷ 365 days/year ≈ 1.9 years.

1b. no; A person who is 1,000,000,000 minutes old would be 1000 × 1.9 ≈ 1900 years old.

2. Someone born 1,000,000 days ago would be 1,000,000 days ÷ 365 days/year ≈ 2740 years old.

3a. It takes a heart about 9.9 days to beat 1,000,000 times: 1,000,000 beats ÷ 70 beats/minute ≈ 14,286 minutes; 14,286 minutes ÷ 60 minutes/hour ≈ 238 hours; 238 hours ÷ 24 hours/day ≈ 9.9 days.

3b. It takes a heart about 1000 × 9.9 = 9900 days, or about 27 years, to beat one billion times.

3c. As 1000 is $\frac{1}{1000}$ of 1,000,000, we can divide 9.9 days by 1000 to find out how long it takes a heart to beat 1000 times. The answer is 0.0099 day, or 0.0099 day × 24 hours/day ≈ 0.238 hour, or 0.238 × 60 minutes/hour ≈ 14.28 minutes. As 1,000,000,000,000 is 1000 times one billion, we can multiply 27 years by 1000 to get 27,000 years.

4a. A billion is 1000 times a million.

4b. A trillion is 1,000,000 times a million.

4c. A trillion is 1000 times a billion.

5a. As 1000 km = 1,000,000 m = 100,000,000 cm, it will take about 100,000,000 ÷ 2 = 50,000,000 pennies.

5b. As 1 mi ≈ 1.6 km, 3000 mi ≈ 4800 km, so it will take about 4.8 × 50,000,000 ≈ 240,000,000 pennies.

6. 5.7×10^9

7. There are about 10,000,000,000 cells in the human brain. Write this number in scientific notation.

In 8–10, use the following table, which shows the monetary cost to the United States of four twentieth-century wars. The figures include the cost to fight the wars and the cost of veterans' benefits paid after the wars.

War	Cost (dollars)
World War I	6.3×10^{10}
World War II	4.48×10^{11}
Korean War	6.7×10^{10}
Vietnam War	1.67×10^{10}

Source: *The World Almanac and Book of Facts 1992.* New York: Pharos Books, 1991, p. 699.

8. Write the costs in standard notation.

9. Calculate the total cost of the four wars, and write the result in both scientific and standard notation.

10. Which war cost the most? Why do you think this war was the most expensive?

Connections

11. Recall that the *prime factorization* of a number is the factor string made up entirely of primes. One way to find the prime factorization of a number is to make a factor tree. The factor tree at right shows that the prime factorization of 20 is $2 \times 2 \times 5$, or $2^2 \times 5$.

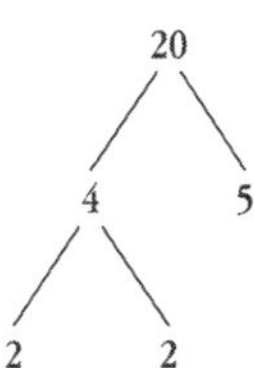

In a–f, write the prime factorization of the number using exponents.

a. 100 **b.** 1000 **c.** 10,000

d. 100,000 **e.** 1,000,000 **f.** 1,000,000,000

g. Look over the prime factorizations you found in parts a–f. What do you notice? Why do you think this happens?

7. 1.0×10^{10}

8. World War I: \$63,000,000,000; World War II: \$448,000,000,000; Korean War: \$67,000,000,000; Vietnam War: \$16,700,000,000

9. 5.947×10^{11} or \$594,700,000,000 (**Teaching Tip:** Some students may have added 6.3, 4.48, 6.7, and 1.67 and affixed a power of 10. To do the addition in this form, the scientific notations must have a common power of 10—for example, by first rewriting the World War II figure as 44.8×10^{10}.)

10. World War II had the greatest cost (the extra factor of 10 is crucial). Probable explanations are duration (though it did not last as long as the Vietnam War), scope (Europe and the Pacific), number of military personnel involved, and benefits paid after the war (the Vietnam War is relatively recent, and there will be more money paid in the future to soldiers who served in Vietnam).

Connections

11a. $100 = 2^2 \times 5^2$

11b. $1000 = 2^3 \times 5^3$

11c. $10{,}000 = 2^4 \times 5^4$

11d. $100{,}000 = 2^5 \times 5^5$

11e. $1{,}000{,}000 = 2^6 \times 5^6$

11f. $1{,}000{,}000{,}000 = 2^9 \times 5^9$

11g. Each number is a multiple of 10, or 2×5. The prime factorization shows the number of 10s that are multiplied, so each exponent equals the number of 0s in the number.

12a. $900 = 9 \times 100 = 3^2 \times 2^2 \times 5^2$

12b. $27{,}000 = 27 \times 1000 = 3^3 \times 2^3 \times 5^3$

12c. $150{,}000 = 15 \times 10{,}000 = 3 \times 5 \times 2^4 \times 5^4 = 2^4 \times 3 \times 5^5$

12d. $24{,}000{,}000 = 24 \times 1{,}000{,}000 = 2^3 \times 3 \times 2^6 \times 5^6 = 2^9 \times 3 \times 5^6$

13a. $2^2 \times 3 \times 5^2 = 3 \times 100 = 300$

13b. $2^2 \times 5^3 = 5 \times 100 = 500$

13c. $2^4 \times 3^2 \times 5^3 = 2 \times 3^2 \times 1000 = 18{,}000$

13d. $2^3 \times 5^4 \times 7 = 5 \times 7 \times 1000 = 35{,}000$

13e. $2^4 \times 3 \times 5^4 \times 7 = 3 \times 7 \times 10{,}000 = 210{,}000$

14a. \$2378.3 million or \$2,378,300,000; $\$2.3783 \times 10^9$ or about $\$2.38 \times 10^9$

14b. \$7535.1 million or \$7,535,100,000; $\$7.5351 \times 10^9$ or about $\$7.54 \times 10^9$

14c. Using a difference, sales in 1990 were nearly \$5.2 billion greater than sales in 1975. Using a quotient, sales in 1990 were more than three times sales in 1975.

12. In a–d, use what you discovered in question 11 to help you find the prime factorization of each number. Write the factorization using exponents.

a. 900 **b.** 27,000

c. 150,000 **d.** 24,000,000

13. In a–e, use what you discovered in questions 11 and 12 to find each product.

a. $2^2 \times 3 \times 5^2$ **b.** $2^2 \times 5^3$ **c.** $2^4 \times 3^2 \times 5^3$

d. $2^3 \times 5^4 \times 7$ **e.** $2^4 \times 3 \times 5^4 \times 7$

In 14–16, use the following table, which shows trends in the value of records, tapes, compact discs (CDs), and music videos sold from 1975 through 1990.

	Value (millions of dollars)			
Music medium	1975	1980	1985	1990
Albums	1485.0	2290.3	1280.5	86.5
Singles	211.5	269.3	281.0	94.4
Eight-track tapes	583.0	526.4	25.3	0
Cassettes	98.8	776.4	2411.5	3472.4
Cassette singles	0	0	0	257.9
Compact discs	0	0	389.5	3451.6
Music videos	0	0	0	172.3

Source: Recording Industry Association of America, as found in the *Statistical Abstract of the United States 1993*. Published by the Bureau of the Census, Washington, D.C., p. 250.

14. **a.** Find the total value of music sold in all media in 1975, and write the result in both scientific and standard notation.

b. Find the total value of music sold in all media in 1990, and write the result in both scientific and standard notation.

c. In a way that makes sense to you, compare the value of music sold in all media in 1990 with that sold in 1975.

15. Describe sales trends of various music media that would have helped an owner of a music store predict sales for 1995.

16. For each year, combine the data for albums and singles to get the value for all records, and combine the data for eight-track tapes, cassettes, and cassette singles to get the value for all audiotapes. Graph the data for records, audiotapes, and CDs on the same coordinate grid. Describe how the value of each medium changed from 1975 through 1990.

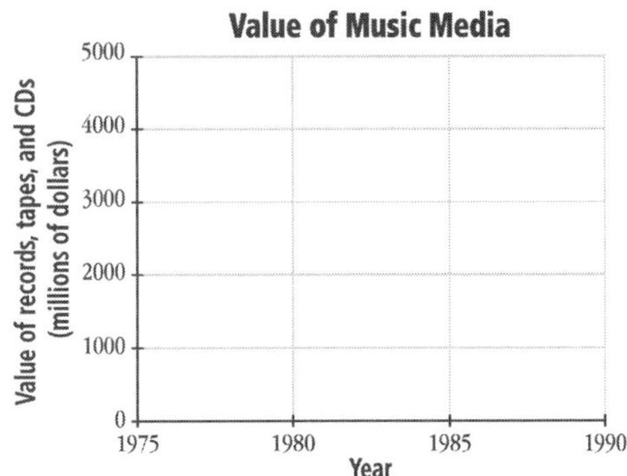

Extensions

17. a. Compute each product mentally.

i. 2000×300 ii. $2000 \times 30{,}000$

iii. 2500×3000 iv. $15{,}000 \times 50{,}000$

b. Describe the strategies you used to compute the products in part a. Can rewriting the factors in scientific notation help you do the mental calculations? If so, explain how.

16.

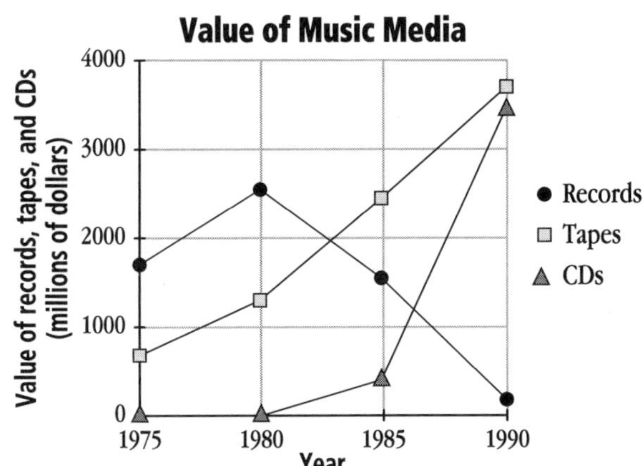

15. Answers will vary, but the obvious trends are a sharp decline in record sales, a sharp increase in CD sales, and continued strong growth of cassette sales.

16. Possible answer: *Records:* In 1975, records represented the greatest share of the market. Sales increased by 1980 and then dropped until 1990, probably because of the introduction of CDs. *Tapes:* The sale of tapes has increased steadily from 1975 to 1990. *CDs:* CDs were not introduced until after 1980. They were slow to catch on until 1985, likely because many people did not have CD players. Sales increased markedly by 1990, almost equaling the sales of tapes. See graph below left. (In the graph, the points are connected to show the trend in the data.)

Extensions

17a. i. 600,000
ii. 60,000,000
iii. 7,500,000
iv. 750,000,000

17b. Students might notice that in products like these, the powers of 10 combine to give a power of 10 that is the sum of the powers and that the other factors multiply separately. You might want to show how this is essentially a commutative rearrangement of the factors. Problem i can be thought of as $(2 \times 10^3) \times (3 \times 10^2) = (2 \times 3) \times (10^3 \times 10^2) = 6 \times 10^5$. Problem iii can be thought of as $(25 \times 10^2) \times (3 \times 10^3) = 75 \times 10^5$.

18a. 4125

18b. 533

In 18 and 19, consider the following information*: In the Northwest, some salmon species migrate up to 900 miles from the Pacific Ocean up rivers in the Columbia River basin to spawning streams to lay their eggs. During the 1950s, about 125,000 adult Snake River chinook salmon returned to their spawning streams in the spring and summer of each year. Because of factors such as dam and reservoir construction, the number of salmon that hatch in the spawning grounds, migrate to the ocean, and return to lay eggs has decreased significantly since the 1950s. During the 1980s, an average of 9600 adult Snake River chinook salmon returned to their spawning streams in the spring and summer of each year.

18. The table below gives the numbers of adult salmon that returned to their spawning streams each year from 1991 through 1994.

Year	Number of salmon
1991	3400
1992	3400
1993	7900
1994	1800

a. What is the mean number of adult salmon that returned each year from 1991 through 1994?

b. What is the average decrease in salmon per year from 1991 through 1994?

*Source: National Marine Fisheries Service

19. a. Two adult salmon produce about 4000 eggs, from which about 800 fry, or baby salmon, hatch. Of these 800 fry, about 200 smolts, or young salmon, survive to migrate to the ocean. What is the survival rate of salmon from eggs to young salmon that migrate to the ocean?

b. How many eggs must be laid to produce a migration of 1 million salmon to the ocean?

20. The table below gives population estimates for major regions of the world. Notice that the estimates are in millions.

Region	Population in 1995 (millions)
Africa	721
Asia	3403
North America	292
Latin America	481
Europe	807
Oceania	29

a. For each population estimate, tell what your calculator display would look like if you entered the number and pressed ENTER.

b. Find the difference between the population of Asia and the population of Africa in two ways: by using the numbers as shown in this table and by first writing the number in standard notation. Explain your results.

19a. The survival rate is 200 young salmon from 4000 eggs, or 1 out of 20, or 5%.

19b. For 1,000,000 salmon to successfully migrate to the ocean, $1,000,000 \times 20 =$ 20,000,000 eggs must be laid.

20a. Possible answer: Africa: 7.21E8, Asia: 3.403E9, North America: 2.92E8, Latin America: 4.81E8, Europe: 8.07E8, Oceania: 2.9E7

20b. Using the numbers in the table, the difference is 2682 million. Using standard notation, the difference is 2,682,000,000. The number in standard notation is 1,000,000 times 2682, because 2682 is the number of millions.

Possible Answers

1a. 10

1b. 10

1c. 1000

1d. 1000

1e. 1000

2. One million seconds is about 11.6 days: 1,000,000 seconds ÷ 60 seconds/minute ≈ 16,667 minutes, and 16,667 minutes ÷ 60 minutes/hour ≈ 278 hours, and 278 hours ÷ 24 hours/day ≈ 11.6 days. One billion seconds is about 31.8 years: 11.6 days × 1000 = 11,600 days, and 11,600 days ÷ 365 days/year ≈ 31.8 years. One trillion seconds is about 31.8 years × 1000 = 31,800 years.

3. The calculator uses scientific notation when the number is too large (or too small) to fit in the display window.

4. Scientific notation can be useful when you are working with numbers that are very large, as encountered in population data, government budgets, and numbers in astronomy and physics.

Mathematical Reflections

In this investigation, you developed a sense of how many a million, a billion, and a trillion are, and you learned how to use scientific notation to write large numbers. These questions will help you summarize what you have learned:

1. As you built or imagined larger and larger collections of unit cubes in Problem 4.2, you probably noticed some important connections between numbers.
   - **a.** How many tens are in a hundred?
   - **b.** How many hundreds are in a thousand?
   - **c.** How many thousands are in a million?
   - **d.** How many millions are in a billion?
   - **e.** How many billions are in a trillion?
2. Describe how you can make sense of how many a million, a billion, or a trillion is.
3. When does your calculator display a number in scientific notation?
4. Describe a situation in which scientific notation may be useful.

Think about your answers to these questions, discuss your ideas with other students and your teacher, and then write a summary of your findings in your journal.

Tips for the Linguistically Diverse Classroom

Diagram Code The Diagram Code technique is described in detail in *Getting to Know Connected Mathematics*. Students use a minimal number of words and drawings, diagrams, or symbols to respond to questions that require writing. Example: Question 3—A student might answer this question by drawing a calculator and writing a number on it that has too many digits to fit in the display.

TEACHING THE INVESTIGATION

4.1 • Thinking Big

The meaning of a large number is relative to the context in which it occurs. A yearly salary of $1 million is quite a lot in our current economy, though not rare in the professional sports and entertainment industries; and the U.S. government spends nearly $3 million every minute of every year. This problem provides students with manageable contexts in which to explore the meaning of one million.

Launch

Use the headline that accompanies the problem to begin a discussion of the meaning of one million.

> Think about times you have heard numbers in millions used to describe a situation. What examples can you think of?

Students may know that a landmark for musicians is to sell one million recordings. Some fund-raising events have the raising of one million dollars as a goal.

In Problem 4.2, students will consider even greater numbers. Encourage them now to start looking for and bringing in examples of the use of numbers in millions, billions, and trillions.

Focus the class's attention on the contexts presented in Problem 4.1. Start students thinking about the problem by asking them to brainstorm ways to address each question, but leave the majority of the work and thinking for them to do during the exploration of the problem.

> Make a prediction for each situation. How might you go about answering each of these questions?

Have students work on the problem and follow-up in groups of three or four.

Explore

Once students are in their groups, encourage them to determine what they need to know to complete each part of the problem. Groups may want to brainstorm about each part and then have different members of the group work on selected parts. If they use this approach, remind them that they must share their work and strategies with the others in the group and that all members must understand how to solve each part and agree on the group's answers.

Summarize

Have groups report their solutions, and allow time for their classmates to add other ideas about how to find the solutions.

Here are some strategies students have used to reason about these problems:

- John's group: "We each took our pulse for 15 seconds and then averaged our data. We found that our hearts beat about 17 times in 15 seconds, so that's about 68 beats per minute. We then divided 1,000,000 by 68 to find how many minutes it would take a heart to beat a million times."
- Shamariah's group: "We found the volume of the cookie bag, 1440 cubic centimeters, by multiplying the three dimensions. With 1000 chips in a bag, you need 1000 bags to have a million chips, so we multiplied the volume by 1000 and found that we needed 1,440,000 cubic centimeters. Our classroom is 20 meters by 20 meters by 8 meters, and 20 meters is 2000 centimeters, so the class is 2000 centimeters by 2000 centimeters by 800 centimeters and has a volume of 3,200,000,000 cubic centimeters. So the cookies would fit for sure."
- Luke's group: "We first thought about how many days 1,000,000 hours is. Since there are 24 hours in a day, we divided 1,000,000 by 24 and found that this is about 41,667 days. Then we divided by 365, the number of days in most years, which gave us about 114 years."
- Celia's group: "On the floor, we marked a square 1 meter by 1 meter, which is 10,000 square centimeters. Then, we tried to see how many of us could stand in it. We figured that we would need 100 of these squares, so we multiplied the number of people we had in the square by 100."

Ask students whether they know anyone who is 1,000,000 hours (about 114 years) old. Books of world records will contain the names of a few people who have lived that long.

Once students have talked about each part of the problem, have them share their other "one million" questions from the follow-up. Students do not need to answer these questions, but they may want to make reasonable predictions about the answers.

4.2 • Thinking Even Bigger

In this problem, students work with unit cubes to help them visualize physical representations of large numbers. The growth of the cube configurations emphasizes the magnitude of one million and one billion and, more importantly, reminds students of the crucial fact that each place value is ten times that of the place directly to the right.

Launch

Begin with a short discussion of things involving millions, billions, or trillions. Students might mention figures they have heard on the news, such as salaries of athletes or entertainers, federal-budget figures, or distances to the planets and stars. Don't spend a great deal of time deciding whether the numbers are accurate, but do ask whether the amounts seem reasonable and where students encountered their information. This raises the issue that information from various sources comes with varying degrees of trustworthiness. Some reported numbers are accurate; others are ballpark figures.

For the Teacher: Modeling Large Numbers

Students will need unit cubes to experiment with in this problem. In addition, if possible, obtain complete sets of base ten blocks—including unit cubes (ones), longs (tens), flats (hundreds), and blocks (thousands)—perhaps borrowing them from an elementary school colleague.

If base ten blocks are not available, you might have students cut out longs, flats, and super cubes from Labsheet 4.2 and tape them together to build some of the larger configurations discussed in the problem. If you must use paper models, you may want to do this problem as a class activity and make one construction for each part of Problem 4.2.

Another way to help students to think about how many unit cubes it would take to make the progressively larger figures is to have them think of the unit cubes as centimeter cubes and use metersticks to mark space in the room large enough to hold each figure.

You might also suggest that students visualize that a unit cube is now a super cube, and have them think about putting these "super cubes" together.

To introduce the problem, conduct a class demonstration using a set of base ten blocks, if you have one. Begin by introducing the small cubes as the unit of measure. Put ten unit cubes in a row, and demonstrate that this construction is equal to one long. Show how ten longs can be put together to equal one flat.

If I stack ten flats together, what shape would I get? *(a large cube—a super cube)*

If I put ten super cubes together in the same way that I put ten unit cubes together, what shape would I get? *(a rectangular solid—a super long)*

If you do not have enough blocks to make more than one super long, leave it on display for the class to see.

Next, introduce the questions that are asked in the problem.

How many unit cubes make a long? How many make a flat? How many make a super cube? Problem 4.2 asks you to answer these questions and others. Use your base ten blocks to help you. We don't have enough blocks to build all of the configurations, so you will have to find ways in your group to think about what these new shapes would look like and how many unit cubes would be needed to build each of them.

Have students work in groups of two or three on the problem and follow-up.

Explore

Encourage students to build a model, or part of a model, or to make a sketch for each answer. They don't need to draw all the lines, but they should indicate the dimensions of the larger cubes or longs and indicate how many unit cubes are contained in each configuration.

Summarize

Ask students how they determined the number of unit cubes in each figure in the problem and follow-up, encouraging them to offer more than one strategy for determining the number of cubes. Look for connections to volume; some students may have focused on the dimensions of a figure, multiplying them to compute the volume.

It is important to help students to summarize what they know about place value at this point. They have been asked to identify the number of unit cubes that are needed to make each successively larger configuration. Review the place-value chart from the beginning of Investigation 3, and ask the class how the chart relates to the number of unit cubes needed to make each shape. The illustration below is reproduced on Transparency 4.2B.

Why do the numbers of cubes in the arrangements we've investigated match the numbers on the place-value chart?

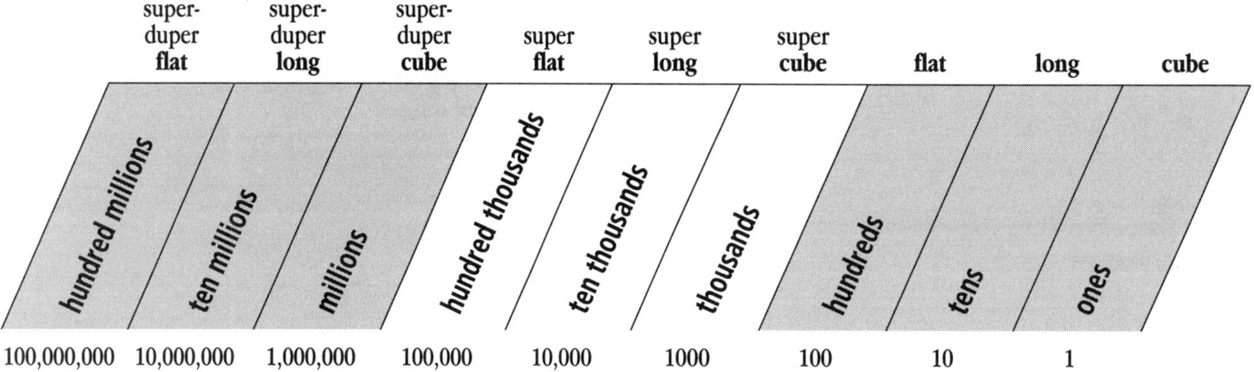

Help students to see the patterns in the chart. The blocks are shaped into cubes, longs, and flats; these shapes occur in a regular cycle, with the shapes growing proportionally larger in each cycle. The cycles represent the places of thousand (super cubes), million (super-duper cubes), and billion (extra-super-duper cubes). Ask questions to help students extend their understanding of place value and large numbers.

How many ones are in ten thousand? How do you know?

How many tens are in ten thousand? How do you know?

How many hundreds are in ten thousand? How do you know?

How many one thousands are in ten million? How do you know?

How many ten thousands are in ten million? How do you know?

How many hundred thousands are in ten million? How do you know?

4.3 • Using Scientific Notation

This problem will help students to develop an understanding of the ways that exponents are used to write large numbers in scientific notation.

Launch

Begin the discussion by talking with students about the problem introduction. Use the examples presented in the "Think about this!" feature in the student edition to open a discussion about scientific and calculator notation.

> Try entering 25,000,000,000,000 on your calculators. Think about the meaning of what you see in the display. Does anyone have any ideas about what the calculator display means?

At this point, students may not have any ideas. You are posing the question to model the kind of reasoning one might employ to approach such problems and to start students thinking about what the symbolic notation might mean.

As students try each of the remaining examples, ask what they think the resulting display means. They will likely have a variety of conjectures, some correct and some incorrect. Ask them to explain their reasoning, and then ask:

> How could you test your ideas with a different example?

Here are some results students may obtain in this exercise:

- When students try to enter 25 trillion on a simple scientific calculator, the calculator will probably stop accepting digits after 25,000,000 or 2,500,000,000. A graphing calculator will accept all 14 digits and, when [ENTER] is pressed, will probably display something like [2.5E13].
- When students try to calculate 500,000 × 500,000, scientific and graphing calculators will probably display something like [2.5E11] or [2.5 11].
- When students enter 10 [^] 5 on a graphing calculator, the result will be 100,000; 10 [^] 8 will result in 100,000,000; and 10 [^] 12 will likely result in [1E12]. When they enter 10 [y^x] 5 on a scientific calculator, the result will be 100,000; 10 [y^x] 8 will likely result in 100,000,000 or [1. 08]; and 10 [y^x] 12 will likely result in [1. 12].

Once students have experimented and understand how to enter exponents into their calculators, begin to explain calculator and scientific notation for large numbers. You might use the information in the student edition to guide your explanation.

Add additional examples if students still seem confused or if you want to check their understanding. For example, ask students to write 600,000 using scientific notation, or to write 8×10^4 or 6.3×10^6 in standard notation.

When you feel that the class has some understanding of the various types of notation, have students work in pairs on the problem.

Explore

Encourage students to help each other by checking answers and by sharing what they know about their calculators.

Students may find part E difficult. On a TI-80 graphing calculator, the display `1.7E12` can be produced in several ways; for example:

- By using the EE key, obtained by pressing [2nd] and then [,]
- By keying in the numeral using standard notation and pressing [ENTER]
- By entering 1.7×10 [^] 1

Save the follow-up questions for the summary.

Summarize

Review the answers for each part of the problem. Take time with part E; students will have found more than one way to obtain each display. Encourage them to explain how they produced the indicated displays.

When you are confident that students have made sense of the ideas in the problem, assign the follow-up questions. Have students work individually and then share ideas with their partners. Follow-up question 1 will help them make connections between standard and scientific notation for writing large numbers; questions 2 through 5 can serve as a checkpoint to assess students' knowledge.

When you review follow-up question 3, it is best to focus on the meaning of multiplication. If you get into rules about adding zeros or moving decimal points, be sure to also discuss why the rules work and what adding zeros means.

You might ask students to propose numbers written in one of the three notations—standard, scientific, or calculator—and challenge the class to translate them into the other notations. For example:

> How do you write 314,000 in scientific notation? In calculator notation?
>
> How do you write 2.718×10^8 in calculator notation? In standard notation?

If students need more practice, offer a few other problems, such as the following:

> Write these numbers in standard notation: 2.8×10^6 *(2,800,000)*, 3.602×10^9 *(3,602,000,000)*, 2.03×10^8 *(203,000,000)*, 9.072×10^2 *(907.2)*.
>
> Write these numbers in scientific notation: 1,462,000,000 *(1.462×10^9)*, 42,023,000 *(4.2023×10^7)*, 94,000,000,000 *(9.4×10^{10})*, 208,000,000 *(2.08×10^8)*, 600,588,000,000,000,000,000,000 *(6.00588×10^{23})*.
>
> Write these numbers as powers of 10: 1,000,000 *(10^6)*, 10,000,000,000 *(10^{10})*.

Additional Answers

Answers to Problem 4.3 Follow-Up

3. To translate a number from scientific notation to standard notation, you multiply the first number by the number of 10s indicated by the exponent. For example, to translate 4×10^{13} into standard notation, you multiply 4 by thirteen 10s, or $4 \times$ 10,000,000,000,000, which is 40,000,000,000,000. For 3.5×10^7, you multiply 3.5 by seven 10s, or $3.5 \times 10{,}000{,}000$, which is 35,000,000.

4. To translate a number from standard notation to scientific notation, you write the number in factored form using only 10s and one other number greater than or equal to 1 and less than 10. For example, to translate 32,000,000 into scientific notation, you write $3.2 \times 10 \times 10 \times 10 \times 10 \times 10 \times 10 \times 10$, or 3.2×10^7.

Every Litter Bit Hurts

The problems in this investigation focus on how individual instances of pollution and litter can lead to enormous environmental problems. Students work with data that are expressed as wholes and as rates, and they use rates and ratios to explore large numbers. In the process, they review some of the ideas they encountered in the *Comparing and Scaling* unit.

In Problem 5.1, Going Hog Wild, students use given rates of increase to predict hog populations in North Carolina counties in the year 2003. In Problem 5.2, Recycling Cans, they determine the number of soft drink cans used in a day by their class and then use this rate to predict the number used by the school and the entire United States in a day, a week, and a year. In Problem 5.3, Going Down the Drain, students determine the typical amount of water that they would use if they were to leave the faucet running while they brushed their teeth, and then they use this rate to calculate the amount of water that would be used by the entire U.S. population for this purpose in a year. In Problem 5.4, Making Mountains out of Molehills, students use information about the average amount of garbage generated per person per day to estimate the volume of compacted waste produced in the United States each day.

Mathematical and Problem-Solving Goals

- ***To further develop operation sense, the ability to choose the numbers and operations needed to answer specific questions from given information***
- ***To investigate how small quantities can accumulate to produce a large quantity***

Materials

Problem	For students	For the teacher
All	Graphing calculators	Transparencies 5.1 to 5.4 (optional), overhead graphing calculator (optional)
5.4	Yardsticks (1 per group)	Cardboard boxes approximately 1-foot square or with dimensions that represent combinations of 1-foot-square boxes, such as 1 foot by 2 feet by 1 foot (optional)

Student Pages 51–60 Teaching the Investigation 60a–60g

INVESTIGATION 5

Every Litter Bit Hurts

Sometimes data are reported as *totals.* In Investigation 3, you looked at the total number of people in 20 major metropolitan areas. At other times, data are given as *rates.* In Problem 3.4, you looked at the number of hogs per square mile. In this investigation, you will continue work with data given in both forms, and you will see how you can scale rate data to find useful information.

5.1 Going Hog Wild

In Problem 3.4, you looked at data for the 15 North Carolina counties that had the greatest 1993 hog populations. In this problem, you will work with the data from the top 5 counties.

County	1993 hog population	Growth from 1983	Hogs per square mile
Sampson	1,152,000	363%	1218
Duplin	1,041,000	349%	1273
Wayne	333,000	265%	603
Bladen	271,000	1178%	310
Greene	231,000	82%	870

Source: U.S. Department of Agriculture, as reported in the *Raleigh News and Observer,* 19–26 February 1995.

Did you know?

- Hogs are one of the most intelligent domesticated animals.
- Hogs have no sweat glands and wallow in the mud to keep cool.
- Hogs weigh about 2.5 pounds at birth. When fully grown, boars (male hogs) may weigh more than 500 pounds.
- Hogs have very poor eyesight but a very keen sense of smell.
- Scientists believe that people began domesticating hogs about 8000 years ago.

Tips for the Linguistically Diverse Classroom

Visual Enhancement The Visual Enhancement technique is described in detail in *Getting to Know Connected Mathematics.* It involves using real objects or pictures to make information more comprehensible. Example: When discussing the introduction to Going Hog Wild and the information in the "Did you know?" feature, you might display a map of North Carolina and show pictures of hogs keeping cool in the mud and fully grown boars.

Going Hog Wild

At a Glance

Grouping: groups of 2 or 3

Launch

- Ask questions to help students think about how to work with percents greater than 100%.
- Have students work in groups of two or three on the problem and follow-up.

Explore

- Suggest that groups record their work in a table. *(optional)*
- Help students who are having trouble first estimate the 2003 population.
- Assist students who forget to add the original population to the growth in the population.

Summarize

- Discuss the answers to the problem and follow-up, having students explain their reasoning.

Assignment Choices

ACE questions 4, 6–8, and unassigned choices from earlier problems

5.2 Recycling Cans

At a Glance

Grouping:* *groups of 2 or 3

Launch

- As a class, conduct a survey of the number of cans students use in a typical week, make a line plot, and compute the mean and the median and decide which to use.
- Have groups finish the questions and the follow-up.

Explore

- Give groups the number of students in the school, or help them to estimate it.

Summarize

- Have students share their answers and reasoning for the problem and follow-up.
- Help the class make other estimates. *(optional)*
- To prepare for Problem 5.3, ask students to collect data as described in that problem.

Problem 5.1

Assume the growth of the hog populations continues at the rates given in the table for the ten years from 1993 to 2003.

A. Predict the number of hogs in each county at the end of the year 2003. Which counties will have over a million hogs?

B. Will the ranking of these five counties be the same in 2003 as it was in 1993? Explain your answer.

Problem 5.1 Follow-Up

A square mile is about 640 acres. Find the number of hogs per acre for each county in 1993.

5.2 Recycling Cans

Do you recycle your aluminum soft drink cans? You might think that recycling the small number of cans you use won't make a difference. But what if everyone reasoned this way?

Problem 5.2

A. Take a class survey, asking each student to estimate the number of soft drink cans he or she uses in a typical week. Make a line plot of the data, and find the mean and the median.

B. Estimate the number of cans used by all the students in your class in one day, one week, one month, and one year.

C. Estimate the number of cans used by all the students in your school in one day, one week, one month, and one year.

D. Estimate the number of cans used by all 260,000,000 Americans in one day, one week, one month, and one year.

Problem 5.2 Follow-Up

1. It takes about 20 soft drink cans to make 1 pound of recycled aluminum. There are 2000 pounds in a ton. Based on your estimates from Problem 5.2, how many tons of recycled aluminum would be produced each year if Americans recycled all their soft drink cans?

Assignment Choices

ACE questions 1, 2, 5, and unassigned choices from earlier problems (Also, students need to collect data for Problem 5.3; see part A of that problem.)

Answers to Problem 5.1

A. Sampson: 5,334,000; Duplin: 4,674,000; Wayne: 1,215,000; Bladen: 3,463,000; Greene: 420,000; All but Greene County will have over a million hogs.

B. The rankings are not the same. Bladen County moves from fourth place to third because of its enormous growth rate of 1178%.

Answer to Problem 5.1 Follow-Up

Sampson: 1218 ÷ 640 = 1.90; Duplin: 1273 ÷ 640 = 1.99; Wayne: 603 ÷ 640 = 0.94; Bladen: 310 ÷ 640 = 0.48; Greene: 870 ÷ 640 = 1.36

Answers to Problem 5.2

See page 60g.

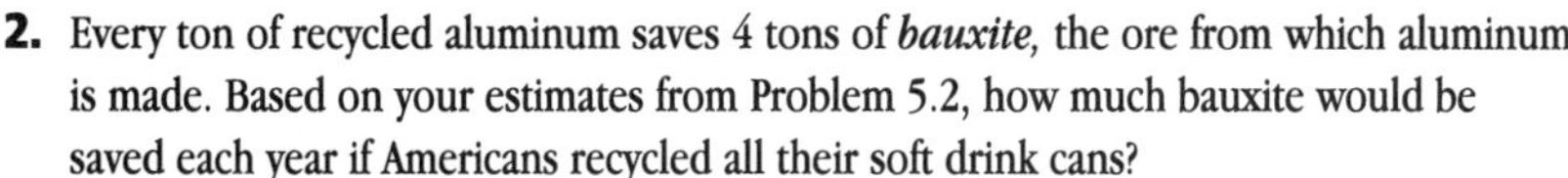

2. Every ton of recycled aluminum saves 4 tons of *bauxite,* the ore from which aluminum is made. Based on your estimates from Problem 5.2, how much bauxite would be saved each year if Americans recycled all their soft drink cans?

5.3 Going Down the Drain

In some countries, droughts make water very precious. In the Middle East and North Africa, water is always in short supply.

Do you leave the water running while you brush your teeth? It may seem that this would not waste much water. In this problem you will investigate how these small amounts of water can add up.

Problem 5.3

A. Time yourself as you brush your teeth, and record the total brushing time. Then, let the water run from the faucet into a large pan for 10 seconds. Use a measuring cup to find the amount of water collected. Use these data to figure out how much water you would use if you let the water run while you brushed your teeth.

B. Collect the data for the entire class on the board, and then find the average amount of water used per student.

C. Suppose everyone let the water run while brushing their teeth. Estimate the amount of water used by your class for toothbrushing in a typical year. Assume each student brushes twice a day. Extend your estimate to find the amount of water that would be used yearly by all 260,000,000 Americans just for toothbrushing.

Problem 5.3 Follow-Up

Estimate the amount of water you would save if you used only enough water to wet and rinse your toothbrush and to rinse your mouth after brushing. Compare this figure with the "let it run" estimate you made in part A.

5.3 Going Down the Drain

At a Glance

***Grouping:* pairs**

Launch

- Prepare a class chart for students to record the data they collected at home.
- As a class, prepare a display of the data, determine the mean and the median, and decide which to use in the calculations.
- Have students work in pairs on the remaining questions and the follow-up.

Explore

- Circulate as students work, helping anyone who is having trouble.

Summarize

- Have students share their estimates and their strategies.
- Help the class make sense of the large numbers.

Answers to Problem 5.2 Follow-Up

1. To get an estimate of the number of tons of aluminum that could be recycled by all Americans in a year, divide the result in part D by 20 to find the number of pounds and then by 2000 to find the number of tons: $(108{,}160{,}000{,}000 \div 20) \div 2000 \approx$ 2,704,000 tons of aluminum.
2. To estimate the bauxite savings, multiply the number of tons of aluminum recycled by 4: $2{,}704{,}000 \times 4 \approx 10{,}816{,}000$ tons of bauxite.

Answers to Problem 5.3

See page 60g.

Answer to Problem 5.3 Follow-Up

See page 60g.

Assignment Choices

ACE question 3 and unassigned choices from earlier problems

Making Mountains out of Molehills

At a Glance

Grouping:* *pairs

Launch

- Ask the class to estimate how much trash Americans produce in one day.
- Have the class make necessary measurements of the classroom for the follow-up.
- Have pairs work on the problem and follow-up.

Explore

- Let students experiment with cube models to get a sense of how the cubes relate to the classroom in size. *(optional)*
- Help students estimate the volume of the school. (optional)

Summarize

- Talk about groups' estimates of the classroom.
- Have groups share and explain their responses to the problem and follow-up.

5.4 Making Mountains out of Molehills

Soft drink cans are only part of the American trash-disposal problem. Families, businesses, and factories produce many other waste materials. In 1988, the U.S. government estimated that the waste from American households and small businesses or industries, called *municipal waste,* amounts to about 4 pounds per person per day.* This may not seem like much, but remember, there are about 260 million Americans!

Problem 5.4

Suppose municipal waste could be compacted into cubes measuring 1 foot on each edge. Each such cube would be composed of about 50 pounds of waste.

If all the municipal waste collected from American homes, businesses, and industries were pressed into 1-foot waste cubes, how many cubes would be produced in just one day?

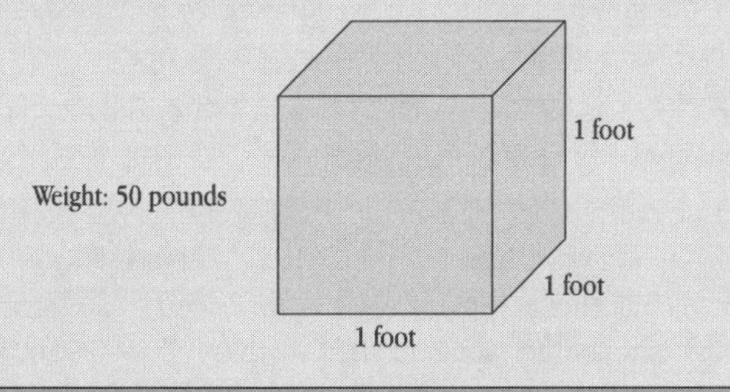

Problem 5.4 Follow-Up

Would the waste cubes produced by Americans in one day fit in your classroom? In your school?

*Source: *Facing America's Trash: What's Next for Municipal Solid Waste?* U.S. Congress OTA. Washington, D.C.: U.S. Government Printing Office, 1989.

Assignment Choices

ACE questions 9, 10, and unassigned choices from earlier problems (Students will need an atlas or almanac for 10.)

Assessment

It is appropriate to use the quiz after this problem.

Answer to Problem 5.4

Americans would produce $260{,}000{,}000 \times 4 \div 50 \approx 20{,}800{,}000$ waste cubes per day.

Answer to Problem 5.4 Follow-Up

In a 20-foot-by-30-foot classroom, 600 cubes would fit in a layer on the floor. If the classroom were 10 feet high, 10 layers of cubes would fit in the room, for a total of $600 \times 10 = 6000$ cubes. The daily American waste would fill roughly $20{,}800{,}000 \div 6000 = 3470$ classrooms of this size. If the school contains 30 classrooms, plus hallways and additional rooms, the waste would fill about 100 schools.

Applications • Connections • Extensions

As you work on these ACE questions, use your calculator whenever you need it.

Applications

In 1–4, use the following facts about recycling.*

- People in the United States use about 50 million tons of paper, made from 850 million trees, every year.
- The average household throws away 13,000 pieces of paper each year. Most is packaging and junk mail.
- The Sunday papers published in the United States each week use pulp from 500,000 trees. The *New York Times* alone requires paper from 75,000 trees per week to meet the demands of its Sunday publication.

1. **a.** How many pounds of paper are used in the United States every year? (Recall that 1 ton = 2000 pounds.)

b. What is the average number of pounds of paper used per American each year? (Remember, there are about 260 million Americans.)

c. On average, how many pounds of paper are made from one tree?

d. How many trees does it take to make the paper used per American in a year?

2. The 260 million Americans live in 97 million households.

a. What is the average number of people in an American household?

b. How many pieces of paper are thrown away per American in a year?

3. **a.** How many trees are used in one year to make the newsprint for all American Sunday papers?

b. How many trees are used in one year to make the newsprint for just the Sunday *New York Times*?

*Source: Rebecca Stefoff. *Recycling.* New York: Chelsea House, 1991.

Answers

Applications

1a. 50,000,000 tons $\times$ 2000 pounds/ton = 100,000,000,000, or 1.0×10^{11}, pounds per year

1b. 100,000,000,000 pounds $\div$ 260,000,000 people $\approx$ 385 pounds per person

1c. 100,000,000,000 pounds $\div$ 850,000,000 trees $\approx$ 118 pounds per tree

1d. $385 \div 118 \approx 3.3$ trees per person per year

2a. 260,000,000 $\div$ 97,000,000 = $260 \div 97 \approx$ 2.7 people per household

2b. $13{,}000 \div 2.7 \approx 4800$ pieces per person per year

3a. 500,000 trees per week $\times$ 52 weeks per year = 26,000,000 trees per year

3b. 75,000 trees per week $\times$ 52 weeks per year = 3,900,000 trees per year

Connections

4. Below is a table of data from a middle school class showing the water used by each student in one week.

Students' Water Use

Student initials	Gallons per student
RE	380
TW	420
HW	299
WE	334
GK	266
DJ	218
MJ	246
WD	246
MA	241
LR	206
FP	247
HA	197
TB	313
CH	188
ME	231
JW	228
PR	211
NP	273
BH	202
EB	189
PJ	182
HJ	160
HM	185
JZ	247

a. What is the median number of gallons of water used in a week by each student? Use this information to estimate the total number of gallons of water used by all 260,000,000 Americans in a week.

b. What is the mean number of gallons of water used in a week by each student? Use this information to estimate the total number of gallons of water used by all 260,000,000 Americans in a week.

c. How do the mean and median number of gallons used per student compare? Why do you think this is so? How did the difference between the mean and the median affect the estimates you made of the weekly use of water by all 260,000,000 Americans?

5. Rabies is a dangerous disease that can infect people and animals. Since 1990, rabies has been found in large numbers of raccoons in the eastern United States. In two counties in New Jersey, the cost of rabies prevention rose from \$768,488 in 1988 to \$1,952,014 in 1990. In New York State, the number of suspected rabies cases in animals rose from 3000 in 1989 to 12,000 in 1993.

In Europe, rabies in foxes has been controlled by mixing vaccine with bait and leaving the bait for the foxes to eat. In Europe, about 75 million vaccine doses were distributed from 1978 through 1994. Because this method was so successful, it is now being tried with raccoons in the United States.*

a. What was the percent change in the cost of rabies prevention from 1988 to 1990 for the two New Jersey counties mentioned above?

b. On average, how many vaccine doses were distributed per year in Europe from 1978 through 1994?

c. It takes 260 vaccine doses per square mile of land for the vaccine to be effective. If these guidelines were followed in Europe, about how many square miles of land were dosed per year?

*Source: C. E. Ruprecht, et al., "The Ascension of Wildlife Rabies: A Cause for Public Health Concern or Intervention?" *Emerging Infectious Diseases* 1, no. 4 (1995).

Connections

4a. The median amount used per week is 236 gallons, the average of 241 and 231. This can be used to estimate the weekly use by Americans as about $236 \times 260{,}000{,}000 = 6.14 \times 10^{10}$ gallons.

4b. The mean amount used per week is approximately 246 gallons. This can be used to estimate the weekly use by Americans as about $246 \times 260{,}000{,}000 = 6.40 \times 10^{10}$ gallons.

4c. The mean is 10 gallons greater than the median. This difference is due to the few large values in the data, which pull the mean up. The estimate for water use when the mean is used is 2.6×10^9 gallons, or 2.6 billion gallons, greater than when the median is used.

5a. The cost rose [(\$1,952,014 – \$768,488) ÷ \$768,488] × 100% = 154%.

5b. 1978 to 1994 is 17 years, and 75,000,000 doses ÷ 17 years ≈ 4,410,000 doses/year.

5c. 4,410,000 doses ÷ 260 doses/square mile ≈ 17,000 square miles

6a. from greatest to least: Chicago, San Jose, Chattanooga, Austin, Yakima, Hamburg

6b. from greatest to least: Chattanooga, San Jose, Chicago, Austin/Hamburg/Yakima

6c. Students will probably say that waste per person is the most appropriate comparison figure, but thoughtful reasoning about either measure is acceptable.

7. *Austin:* 440,000, four hundred forty thousand; *Chicago:* 5,500,000, five million, five hundred thousand; *Chattanooga:* 710,000, seven hundred ten thousand; *Hamburg:* 9900, nine thousand nine hundred; *San Jose:* 1,600,000, one million, six hundred thousand; *Yakima:* 41,000, forty-one thousand

8. To estimate population, divide total waste by rate per person: *Austin:* 440,000 ÷ 0.9 ≈ 490,000 people; *Chicago:* 5,500,000 ÷ 1.8 ≈ 3,060,000 people; *Chattanooga:* 710,000 ÷ 4.3 ≈ 165,000 people; *Hamburg:* 9900 ÷ 0.9 ≈ 11,000 people; *San Jose:* 1,600,000 ÷ 2.2 ≈ 727,000 people; *Yakima:* 41,000 ÷ 0.9 ≈ 45,600 people

In 6–8, use the following table, which gives information about municipal solid waste produced in six U.S. cities.

Municipal Solid Waste in U.S. Cities, 1989

City	Kilograms per day	Kilograms per day per person
Austin, Texas	4.4×10^5	0.9
Chicago, Illinois	5.5×10^6	1.8
Chattanooga, Tennessee	7.1×10^5	4.3
Hamburg, New York	9.9×10^3	0.9
San Jose, California	1.6×10^6	2.2
Yakima, Washington	4.1×10^4	0.9

Source: *Facing America's Trash: What's Next for Municipal Solid Waste?* U.S. Congress OTA. Washington, D.C.: U.S. Government Printing Office, 1989.

6. **a.** Rank the cities according to the number of kilograms of solid waste produced each day.

b. Rank the cities according to the amount of solid waste produced per person each day.

c. Which measure of solid waste produced seems better for comparing the cities? Explain your choice.

7. Write each amount from the "Kilograms per day" column in standard notation and in words.

8. Estimate the population of each city.

Extensions

In 9 and 10, use the following information: Some of the natural resources we depend on, such as trees and water, are renewable or naturally recycled. Others, such as oil, coal, and gas, are not renewable. Some scientists are urging countries that use natural resources heavily to begin programs of conservation. The table on the following page shows 1989 oil consumption in seven major industrial countries.

1989 Oil Consumption

Country	Oil consumed (barrels)
Britain (England, Scotland, Wales)	6.34×10^8
Canada	6.431×10^8
France	6.774×10^8
West Germany	8.315×10^8
Italy	7.081×10^8
Japan	1.818×10^9
United States	6.324×10^9

9. What do you think is the best way to compare the oil consumption of the United States with the oil consumption of the other countries? Explain your choice.

10. **a.** A barrel of oil holds 42 gallons. For each country listed, calculate the oil consumption in gallons.

b. Find the 1989 populations of the listed countries in an atlas or almanac. Use this information to find the number of gallons of oil consumed per person in 1989 for each country.

c. Using your answer to part b, find the daily oil consumption per person for each country in 1989.

d. Compare the rate of oil consumption in the United States to the rates in the other countries. Explain any differences you find.

Extensions

9. Oil consumption might be compared per person or per square mile of land. Both choices have some drawbacks. For example, the per-person figure does not account for the fact that a country such as Japan, with many people crowded into a small area, will need proportionally less fuel for transportation compared to the sprawling United States or Canada. Also, per-person figures do not take climatic differences into account—countries with warmer climates need less fuel for heating, though perhaps more for air conditioning. On the other hand, greater land area does not necessarily imply a greater share of world resources.

10a–c. See below left.

10d. Possible answer: It is clear that the United States uses more oil per person than any of the other countries listed. Only the consumption rate of Canada, which is similar in geography and climate to the northern United States, comes close to the U.S. consumption rate. All of the other countries probably have a greater population density than the United States and Canada, so they may use less fuel for transportation.

10a–c. **1989 Oil Consumption**

Country	**a.** Oil consumed (gallons)	1989 Population (millions)	**b.** Gallons per person (total)	**c.** Gallons per person (daily)
Britain	2.663×10^{10}	57	467	1.28
Canada	2.701×10^{10}	27	1000	2.74
France	2.845×10^{10}	56	508	1.39
West Germany	3.492×10^{10}	61	572	1.57
Italy	2.974×10^{10}	58	513	1.40
Japan	7.636×10^{10}	124	616	1.69
United States	2.656×10^{11}	250	1062	2.91

Mathematical Reflections

In this investigation, you explored data given both as totals and as rates. For example, in Problem 5.1, you worked with the total hog population and with the number of hogs per square mile. These questions will help you summarize what you have learned:

1 Look back over the problems in this and other investigations.

a. Find examples of data that are expressed as totals and examples of data that are expressed as rates.

b. When you rank a set of data, does it make a difference whether you use the totals or the rates? Explain.

2 **a.** If you are given a total for some group of people or time period, how do you calculate a rate per person or per shorter time period?

b. If you are given a per-person rate or per-time-period rate, how do you calculate the total for a whole group or for a longer time period?

Think about your answers to these questions, discuss your ideas with other students and your teacher, and then write a summary of your findings in your journal.

Possible Answers

1a. Some data in this unit that are expressed as totals are the gallons of oil spilled by the *Exxon Valdez,* the populations of metropolitan areas, and the hog populations in certain counties in North Carolina. Some data in this unit that are expressed as rates are the number of soft drink cans used per person or per school over a given time period, the growth rate in hog populations, and the amount of waste produced per person per day.

1b. It does make a difference whether you use totals or rates when you rank a set of data. For the hog populations, we found a different ranking when we used total population than when we used rate of growth.

2a. To find a rate per person, divide the total for the group by the number of people in the group. To find a rate for the shorter time period, divide the total for the longer time period by the number of units of the shorter time period (seconds, minutes, hours, days, and so on) in the longer time period. We did the second, a rate for a shorter time period, when we looked at our aluminum can data. We found that the median value of cans used per week was 8. The median value of cans used per day would be $8 \div 7 = 1.1$ cans per day.

2b. See page 60g.

Tips for the Linguistically Diverse Classroom

Diagram Code The Diagram Code technique is described in detail in *Getting to Know Connected Mathematics*. Students use a minimal number of words and drawings, diagrams, or symbols to respond to questions that require writing. Example: Question 1a—A student might answer this question by writing the headings *Totals* and *Rates*. Under the *Totals* heading, the student might draw the *Exxon Valdez* and a gallon of oil; a population map with a city's inhabitants indicated by a cluster of dots; and hogs inside county boundary lines in an outline of the state of North Carolina. Under the *Rates* heading, the student might draw a stick figure holding a soft drink can labeled *7 days* and another stick figure standing next to trash can labeled *24 hours*.

5.1 • Going Hog Wild

In this problem, students use growth rates for the North Carolina hog populations from Problem 3.4 to predict hog populations in 2003.

Launch

Have students look back at their work for Problem 3.4. Remind them that they made several comparisons between the various data sets presented in the problem. Explain that they will now revisit a portion of the hog data, focusing this time on the column labeled "Growth from 1983."

What does it mean for a growth rate to be 363% or 349%?

Students may not have much to say about this question at this time, which is fine. The following questions should help them to make sense of the growth rates; you can ask similar questions again after students have explored the problem.

Suppose a certain population has 20 members and a yearly growth rate of 10%. What will the population be at the end of one year? *(22)* How did you compute this? *(by finding 10% of 20 and adding that to the starting population: 20 + 20 × 10% = 22)*

If the population is 20 and the yearly growth rate is 80%, what will the population be at the end of one year? *(20 × 80% + 20 = 36)*

If the population is 20 and the yearly growth rate is 100%, what will the population be at the end of one year? *(20 × 100% + 20 = 40, or double the original)*

If the population is 20 and the yearly growth rate is 200%, what will the population be at the end of one year? *(20 × 200% + 20 = 60)*

What is another way to describe a growth rate of 100%? A growth rate of 200%? *(A growth rate of 100% means the population will double. A growth rate of 200% means the population will triple.)*

Now, ask the class how many hogs there will be in the five counties at the end of the year 2003 if the same rates of growth apply. This is the question posed in Problem 5.1.

Have students work in groups of two or three on the problem and follow-up.

Explore

You may want to suggest that groups record their data in a table such as the one shown below.

County	1993 hog population	2003 hog population
Sampson		
Duplin		
Wayne		
Bladen		
Greene		

If students are struggling with finding the new populations, help them think about first estimating the new populations. Since they know that a growth rate of 100% will cause the population to double, and a growth rate of 200% will cause it to triple, Sampson, Duplin, and Bladen Counties must have 2003 populations that are more than triple their 1993 populations.

Some students may forget to add the original population to the additional population computed from the percent growth. Look for this, and help students understand why this is necessary.

Summarize

Discuss the predicted 2003 hog populations, and review the strategies that groups found helpful. Ask the class whether the rankings of the counties in terms of hog populations remain the same and, if they change, ask for explanations about what caused the changes.

Discuss the follow-up and how students arrived at their answers. Ask students if, based on the number of hogs per acre, they can make a guess about which counties seem to have room for even greater hog populations.

5.2 • Recycling Cans

This problem focuses on the recycling of a common consumer item: soft drink cans. Students are asked to devise a strategy for estimating the number of cans the class uses in a typical day, week, month, and year, and then to extrapolate that estimate to the populations of the school and the entire country.

Launch

As a class, do part A of the problem. Help the class conduct a survey of their weekly use of soft drink cans and display the results in a line plot. Remind students that they are only counting aluminum cans, not soft drinks in 2-liter bottles or other containers. One easy way to construct the line plot is to have each student mark an X for his or her estimated usage above the appropriate number on the scale of a line plot drawn on the board.

Review with students how to find the median and mean of the resulting distribution. The median is the value above and below which half of the data points lie. The mean is calculated by summing all the data entries and dividing by the number of pieces of data. (You may want to review the grade 6 unit *Data About Us* for ideas on how to help students understand the concepts of the median and the mean.)

Ask students which statistic—the mean or the median—seems more typical of the data. Have the class reach a decision on which statistic to use in their work on parts B and C and the follow-up.

Have students work in groups of two or three on the remaining questions in the problem and on the follow-up questions.

Explore

For part B, students will need to work backward from the collected data to estimate the number of cans used in one day.

For part C, groups will need to know the number of students in the school. Either provide them with this number or help the class to make an estimate, perhaps working from an estimate of the number of classes in the school and the average number of students per class.

Students will use their results from part D to answer the follow-up questions. Encourage them to use both scientific and standard notation to record their responses.

Summarize

Ask students to share their responses and reasoning for each part of the problem and for the follow-up questions. Allow enough time for the class to consider the various strategies that are proposed. Then ask:

> How accurate do you think your estimate of the number of soft drink cans you use in one week is?
>
> Is it reasonable to assume that the number of cans we use in our class is a good estimate for the number of cans other students in our school would use? Is it a good estimate for the number of cans the average American would use?

If you and the students wish, the class can make some other estimates, such as the amount of money spent on cans of soda, the number of cases of soda bought, or the number of ounces of soda consumed in a year by the class or by all 260,000,000 Americans. If your state requires bottle deposits, students could estimate the amount of money collected in bottle deposits in a year, then conduct some research to find out what percentage of those deposits are actually returned to consumers.

For the Teacher: Preparing for Problem 5.3

For Problem 5.3, students will need to collect data, in advance, on the amount of water they would waste if they let the faucet run while they brushed their teeth. Ask students to read the directions in part A of Problem 5.3. Talk with them about how to conduct the experiment, and have students collect their data at home.

Discuss the need for everyone to use the same unit to measure the water; in this experiment, they will use a customary measuring cup.

For most experiments, it's a good idea to first make some thoughtful guesses about the likely results. Have students guess how much water they use for brushing their teeth before they collect their data: "I'd like you to think a bit about how much water runs down the drain while you brush your teeth. Record your estimate, and later we will compare it to the experimental data we will collect."

Return to these estimates when students bring in their results, and ask the class to assess how accurate their guesses were.

If you are pressed for time and cannot have the class collect real data, you may want to use 10 cups as a reasonable amount of water that would be collected if the water ran during a thorough toothbrushing.

5.3 • Going Down the Drain

In this problem, students collect some personal data and then extrapolate to a larger population. In a sense, these problems are scaling-up tasks similar to those involving traditional proportional reasoning. However, students will likely find it more natural to use the data they collect here to establish rates and then use multiplication to answer the questions, rather than setting up a classical $a:b = c:d$ proportion.

Launch

Students will need to bring in the data they have collected at home about the amount of water they would use if they let the faucet run while they brushed their teeth. Set up a chart or table on the board, and have each student record his or her information.

Name	Number of seconds brushed	Amount of water used

Then ask:

Why do some of you brush for a similar length of time but use different amounts of water? *(The rate of water flow from the faucets probably differs.)*

How might we organize our data to determine the typical amount of water we would use if we let the faucet run while we brushed our teeth?

Students may suggest organizing the amounts in an ordered list or a line plot. For a continuous variable such as the amount of water collected, a line plot doesn't make much sense as a display. You might suggest that the class group the data in intervals to make a histogram, or simply list all the data in order. Once the display has been constructed, have students determine the mean and the median of the data, and discuss which measure best represents the typical amount of water used by a student in the class.

Have students work in pairs to address the rest of the problem and the follow-up.

Explore

This problem is quite similar to Problem 5.2. Observe pairs as they work, and help anyone who is struggling. You will want to find time and ways to assist those who need help to develop an understanding of the strategies that can be used to solve problems such as these.

Summarize

Ask students to report their estimates. The amount of water used by all Americans for toothbrushing will be a large number and difficult to grasp. Investigation 2 mentions that an Olympic-size swimming pool holds about 500,000 gallons of water. You might use that benchmark to help students make sense of these large numbers. As a class, convert the water usage into gallons (there are 16 cups in a gallon); then, students can estimate the number of swimming pools of water used for toothbrushing by Americans each year. Using 10 cups per brushing as an average, or 20 cups per day per person, gives a total for all Americans of $20 \times 365 \times 260{,}000{,}000 \approx 1.898 \times 10^{12}$ cups, or 1.186×10^{11} gallons, or 237,000 swimming pools full per year! If that doesn't seem significant to the class, ask them to imagine how precious that water would be in one of the desert countries of Africa.

This is a good time to make a connection to linear relationships. For example, if the average amount of water used per brushing is 10 cups, the amount used for n brushings is $10n$. You could make a chart for the water used in the first five or six brushings and ask the class about the relationship. Or, show the linear relationship by sketching a graph.

Number of brushings	Water used (cups)
0	0
1	10
2	20
3	30
4	40
5	50

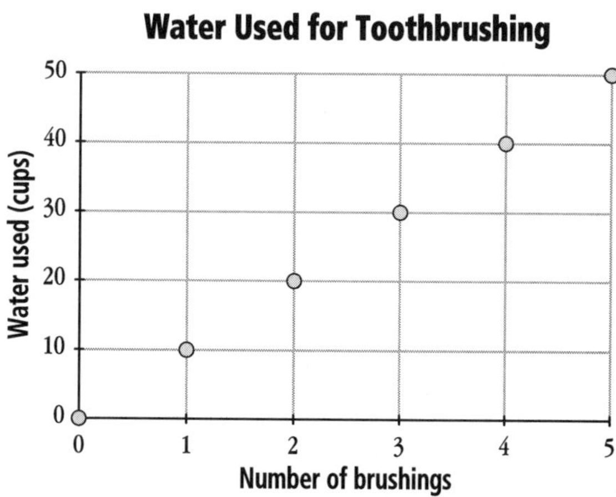

Then ask for an expression that gives the amount of water used by the entire U.S. population after n brushings.

Once the discussion of the problem is complete, talk about the follow-up. You may want to help students translate their answer using the swimming-pool benchmark.

5.4 • Making Mountains out of Molehills

This problem illustrates how small amounts of waste from individual Americans add up to very large amounts for the country as a whole. Students again think about benchmarks that would help them to make sense of the quantities they encounter.

Launch

This problem is similar to Problems 5.2 and 5.3, so students should be able to get to work on it with only a short launch.

Ask students to make a thoughtful estimate of how large a pile of trash would result from collecting all the garbage Americans produce in a single day. Return to their estimate at the end of the problem so that the class can get a sense of their estimating skills in such a situation.

To answer the follow-up question, students will need some measurements of the classroom. Some may already have the length and width of the classroom from their work in Problem 1.2. If so, they will only need to measure the height of the room for this problem. Have students gather what measurement data they need, while you take this opportunity to talk with them informally about accuracy in measurement.

Once students have the measurements they need, have pairs work on the problem and follow-up.

Explore

Models of 1-foot cubes can help students to visualize the problem and to relate the size of a waste cube to their classroom. If you have located cardboard boxes with the dimensions of 1-foot waste cubes or multiples of waste cubes, let students experiment with them. Or, students may want to build models of their own.

This problem requires students to use what they know about volume of a rectangular prism. You may need to review this topic with them.

For the follow-up, students may need assistance estimating the volume of the school.

Summarize

Begin the summary by asking groups for their measurements of the classroom and listing each group's response on the board. Discuss with the class the approximate nature of all measurements.

Have students share their responses to the problem and follow-up. As pairs present their answers and reasoning, allow the class to add other ideas and to raise questions if necessary.

Additional Answers

Answers to Problem 5.2

A. Answers will depend on the class's weekly estimates. The important thing to check is the reasoning that students use to arrive at their answers. Possible line plot:

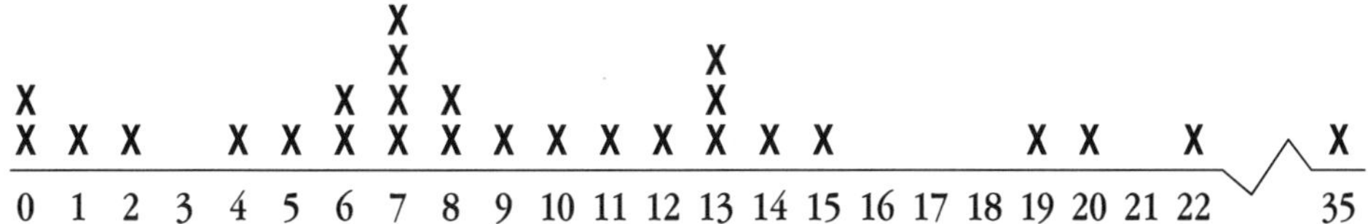

The mean of these data is 10.1 cans per week; the median is 8 cans per week. This class decided that the median was more representative of the data.

B. Using the above data, which involves 27 students and an average of 8 cans per week per student, the estimates are as follows: daily, $(8 \div 7) \times 27 \approx 31$ cans; weekly, $8 \times 27 = 216$ cans; monthly, $30 \times 31 = 930$ cans; yearly, $52 \times 216 = 11{,}232$ cans.

C. The number of students in the school above is 467, so the estimates are as follows: daily, $(8 \div 7) \times 467 \approx 534$ cans; weekly, $8 \times 467 = 3736$ cans; monthly, $30 \times 534 = 16{,}020$ cans; yearly, $52 \times 3736 = 194{,}272$ cans.

D. To obtain estimates for all 260 million Americans, use the median of 8 cans per week: daily, 297 million cans; weekly, 2080 million cans; monthly, 8914 million cans; yearly, 108,160 million cans.

Answers to Problem 5.3

A, B. Answers will vary; however, 10 cups is a reasonable amount.

C. To get a class figure for a year, students must multiply the class average by 2 (for two brushings per day), then by the number of students in the class, and then by 365. To get the usage for all Americans, students must multiply the class average by 2, then by 260,000,000, and then by 365.

Answer to Problem 5.3 Follow-Up

By using water only for wetting and rinsing, the usage will be more like 2 cups per brushing rather than a typical use of 10 cups. (This translates into a savings for the entire United States of about 9.49×10^{10} gallons or 189,800 swimming pools full per year.)

Mathematical Reflections

2b. To find the total for a group, multiply the per-person rate by the number in the group. To find the total for a longer time period, multiply the rate by the number of units of the shorter time period (seconds, minutes, hours, days, and so on) in the longer time period. Again, we can look at our can data to show this first one. We found a median of 8 cans per week. To find the number of cans used in a week by our class, we multiply this by the number of students in class, 27. This gives $8 \times 27 = 216$ cans per week.

On an Average Day

In this final investigation, students use all the strategies they have developed in their preceding work to compare and to make sense of large quantities. They look at data about the United States and Japan and are encouraged to consider which kinds of situations invite comparison by subtraction and which by division. They also revisit the idea of using rates for comparisons, which they encountered in the *Comparing and Scaling* unit.

In Problem 6.1, Recycling Cans, students use addition and subtraction to derive information about recycling in Japan and the United States. Problem 6.2, Making Comparisons in Two Ways, highlights two methods of comparing quantities, subtraction and division. Students will discover that the use of division and multiplication often produces a comparison that makes more sense and better describes the relationship. In Problem 6.3, Comparing by Using Rates, students find that rates produce the most meaningful comparisons of the number of smokers in each country.

Mathematical and Problem-Solving Goals

- ***To make decisions about the best way to compare quantities***
- ***To apply various strategies for writing and comparing quantities***
- ***To use appropriate benchmarks to make sense of large numbers***

Materials

Problem	For students	For the teacher
All	Graphing calculators	Transparencies 6.1 to 6.3 (optional)

Student Pages 61–69 | Teaching the Investigation 69a–70

On an Average Day

Natural disasters and human catastrophes make the headlines in newspapers and on television and radio news broadcasts. But for a majority of people most days are "average" days. In this investigation, you will look at some interesting facts about average days.

The book *On an Average Day in Japan** compares life in the United States with life in Japan. The book contains lots of data about life in the two countries, and you can discover even more information by doing a little arithmetic. Note that this information was collected when the population of the United States was 250,000,000.

6.1 Recycling Cans

On an average day in Japan, about 52,055,000 aluminum cans are used. Japan's population of 123 million people recycles 34,356,000 of those cans. In the United States, which has a population of 250 million people, about 93,310,000 aluminum cans are used on an average day, and about half of them are recycled.

Problem 6.1

A. How many aluminum cans are *not* recycled in Japan on an average day?

B. How many aluminum cans are *not* recycled in the United States on an average day?

C. In an average week, how many aluminum cans are used in each country? How many cans are recycled?

Problem 6.1 Follow-Up

A standard aluminum can is about 12 centimeters tall. If all the cans used in Japan on an average day were stacked in a tower, how tall would the tower be in centimeters? In meters? In kilometers?

*Tom Heyman. *On an Average Day in Japan.* New York: Fawcett Columbine, 1992.

6.1 Recycling Cans

At a Glance

Grouping: individuals or pairs

Launch

- Introduce the topic of aluminum can use in Japan and the United States.
- Read the problem with the class.
- Have students work on the problem and follow-up.

Explore

- If students work individually, use the opportunity to assess their understanding of concepts from this unit.

Summarize

- Ask students for explanations about their answers.
- Have students convert their answers to parts A and B to scientific notation, and talk about which notation is easier for comparing the numbers.
- Discuss the follow-up, and ask what distance students could compare to the tower's height.

Answers to Problem 6.1

A. 17,699,000 cans

B. 46,655,000 cans

C. In an average week in Japan, 364,385,000 cans are used and 240,492,000 are recycled. In the United States, 653,170,000 cans are used and 326,585,000 are recycled.

Answer to Problem 6.1 Follow-Up

The tower would be 624,660,000 cm, 6,246,600 m, or 6246.6 km tall.

Assignment Choices

ACE questions 10, 14–17, and unassigned choices from earlier problems

Making Comparisons in Two Ways

At a Glance

Grouping: groups of 2 or 3

Launch

- Use the examples in the problem introduction to suggest ways to compare numbers.
- If students need more practice, offer another example.
- Have students explore the problem and follow-up in groups of two or three.

Explore

- If groups want to divide the work, remind them to share and agree on each answer.

Summarize

- Have groups present answers for the parts of the problem and explain how they found them.
- Ask the class to summarize the two methods of comparison.
- Let students share their ideas about the follow-up.

6.2 Making Comparisons in Two Ways

There are 250 million people in the United States and 123 million people in Japan. The population of the United States is clearly greater than the population of Japan, but how can you describe how much greater?

You could compare the populations by finding a difference. Since $250 - 123 = 127$, the population of the United States is about 127 million greater than the population of Japan.

You could also compare the populations by figuring out how many times greater the population of the United States is. Since the population of Japan is close to 125 million, and since $250 = 2 \times 125$ (or, equivalently, $250 \div 125 = 2$), the population of the United States is about two times the population of Japan.

Problem 6.2

The following statements give information about life in Japan and the United States. In each case, compare the data for the countries in the two ways described above, and decide which comparison better explains the similarities or differences.

A. The average Japanese child spends 275 hours each year playing sports and games. The average American child spends 550 hours each year in these activities.

B. The average American has $10,000 in savings accounts. The average Japanese has about $40,000 saved.

C. On an average day, Japanese children spend 7 hours in school, and American children spend 5 hours 25 minutes in school.

D. The average American makes 200 telephone calls each month. The average Japanese makes 45 calls each month.

E. On an average day, 40% of Japanese use public transportation, while fewer than 4% of Americans do.

Problem 6.2 Follow-Up

What are some reasons people in the United States and Japan might differ in the ways described in the problem?

Assignment Choices

ACE questions 1–4 and unassigned choices from earlier problems

Answers to Problem 6.2

A. The average American child spends 275 more hours playing sports and games each year than does the average Japanese child, or two times the number of hours.

B. The average Japanese has $30,000 more in savings than does the average American, or four times the savings.

C. See page 70.

D. The average American makes 155 more telephone calls per month than does the average Japanese, or about 4.4 times as many calls.

E. See page 70.

Answer to Problem 6.2 Follow-Up

Answers will vary.

6.3 Comparing by Using Rates

What is the message in the following statement about photography in Japan and the United States?

> Japanese take 714,500,000 pictures every month, and Americans take 1,250,200,000 pictures every month.

You might conclude that Americans take many more pictures than do Japanese, but remember that the population of the United States is about twice that of Japan.

One way to make a fair comparison in this kind of situation is to calculate a *rate*. In this case, you could find the number of pictures taken per person. In Japan, this rate is as follows:

714,500,000 pictures ÷ 123,000,000 people ≈ 6 pictures per person

In the United States, this rate is as follows:

1,250,200,000 pictures ÷ 250,000,000 people ≈ 5 pictures per person

This comparison tells a different story than does the total number of pictures. Although the number of pictures taken in the United States is greater than the number of pictures taken in Japan, Japanese take more pictures per person.

Problem 6.3

The table below gives some data about smoking in the United States and Japan.

Country	Population	Smokers	Total cigarettes smoked each day
United States	250,000,000	55,000,000	1,437,315,000
Japan	123,000,000	33,000,000	849,315,000

A. Compare the number of smokers in the two countries in as many ways as you can. Which comparison do you believe is best?

B. Compare the number of cigarettes smoked each day in the two countries in as many ways as you can. Which comparison do you believe is best?

Problem 6.3 Follow-Up

Would you say that smoking is more widespread in the United States or in Japan? Explain your reasoning.

Comparing by Using Rates

At a Glance

Grouping: pairs

Launch

- As a class, explore the questions posed in the problem introduction.
- Have students work in pairs on the problem and follow-up.

Explore

- Make sure students are finding per-person rates as one type of comparison.

Summarize

- Have students offer their comparisons and discuss their strengths and weaknesses.
- Talk about the follow-up question.

Answers to Problem 6.3

A. Possible answer: There are 22 million more smokers in the United States than in Japan. There are 1.7 times (55 million ÷ 33 million) as many smokers in the United States as in Japan. Also, 22% ($\frac{55}{250}$) of Americans smoke, while 27% ($\frac{33}{123}$) of Japanese smoke. The percentage comparison is best, because it tells more directly how the two populations compare.

B. See page 70.

Answer to Problem 6.3 Follow-Up

Answers will vary. Some students will compare the numbers of smokers and say that there is more smoking in the United States. Others will point to the ratios of smokers to the total population, and say that there is more smoking in Japan. Some will use the data about the number of cigarettes smoked per person per day, which indicate that smoking is slightly more widespread in the United States.

Assignment Choices

ACE questions 5–9, 11–13, and unassigned choices from earlier problems (Students need an atlas for 12.)

Answers

Applications

1. Possible answer: Robert Wadlow was 7 ft 0.5 in (215 cm) taller than Gul Mohammed. Wadlow was about 4.8 times as tall as Mohammed. (With sound reasoning, students may support any comparison.)

2. Possible answer: Jon Minnoch weighed 1277 lb (580 kg) more than his wife. Jon Minnoch weighed about 12.6 times as much as his wife.

3. Possible answer: The Rutan/Yeager flight took nearly 76 days less than the *Triton* submarine trip. The *Triton* submarine took more than 9 times as long to travel around the world as did the Rutan/Yeager flight.

4. Possible answer: The largest hamburger had a diameter 101 ft 8 in (31 m) less than that of the largest pizza. The pizza's diameter was almost 6 times that of the hamburger, and the pizza's area was about 34 times that of the hamburger.

5a. 30,000 km/h × 24 h = 720,000 km

5b. 800,000 km ÷ 30,000 km/h ≈ 26.7 h

Applications • Connections • Extensions

As you work on these ACE questions, use your calculator whenever you need it.

Applications

In 1–4, compare the given measurements in two ways, and tell which of the two comparisons you think is better.*

1. The tallest man in medical history is Robert Wadlow, who was measured at 8 feet 11 inches (272 centimeters) shortly before his death in 1940. The shortest adult in history is Gul Mohammed of Delhi, India. In 1990, he was measured at $22\frac{1}{2}$ inches (57 centimeters).

2. The heaviest person in medical history is Jon Minnoch, who reached a weight of 1387 pounds (630 kilograms). Minnoch's wife weighed 110 pounds (50 kilograms).

3. In 1960, the U.S. navy submarine *Triton* traveled around the world in 84 days 19 hours. In 1986, Richard Rutan and Jeana Yeager became the first aviators to fly around the world without refueling, taking 9 days 3 minutes 44 seconds.

4. The largest hamburger on record was made at a county fair in Wisconsin in 1989. It weighed 5520 pounds (2509 kilograms) and had a diameter of 21 feet (6.4 meters). The largest pizza was baked at a market in South Africa in 1990. It had a diameter of 122 feet 8 inches (37.4 meters) and an area of 11,818 square feet (1098 square meters).

5. A NASA space shuttle travels about 30,000 kilometers per hour.

a. How far will the shuttle travel in one day?

b. How long would it take the shuttle to travel to the moon and back, a distance of about 400,000 kilometers each way?

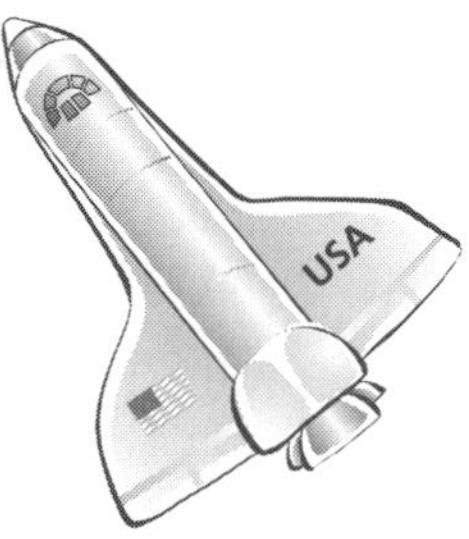

*Source: *Guinness Book of Records 1994.* Ed. Peter Matthews. New York: Bantam Books, 1994.

6. A typical human heart beats about 70 times per minute.

   a. How many times does a typical heart beat in an hour?

   b. How many times does a typical heart beat in a day?

   c. How many times does a typical heart beat in a year?

7. There are about 3,225,000 12-year-olds in the United States.

   a. About how many Americans will celebrate their thirteenth birthday each day of the coming year?

   b. How many candles will be needed for all Americans who celebrate their thirteenth birthdays this year if each person has a cake with 13 candles?

   c. If there are 24 candles per box, how many boxes of candles will be needed for all the thirteenth-birthday cakes this year?

8. On an average day, Americans spend $945,111,233 for food.

   a. How much is this per person per day?

   b. How much is this per person per year?

Connections

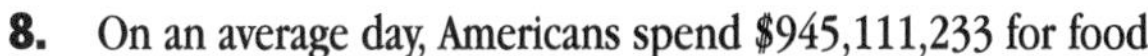

9. Reports from the Soviet Union, just before it broke into smaller countries in 1991, claimed that on an average day about 70 million Soviet citizens smoked cigarettes at a rate of three cigarettes per smoker.* How many cigarettes were smoked on an average day in the former Soviet Union?

*Source: Tom Heymann. *On an Average Day in the Soviet Union.* New York: Fawcett Columbine, 1990.

6a. $70 \times 60 = 4200$ beats per hour

6b. $4200 \times 24 = 100{,}800$ beats per day

6c. $100{,}800 \times 365 = 36{,}792{,}000$ beats per year

7a. $3{,}225{,}000 \div 365 \approx 8836$ Americans

7b. $3{,}225{,}000 \times 13 = 41{,}925{,}000$ candles

7c. $41{,}925{,}000 \div 24 \approx 1{,}746{,}900$ boxes

8a. $\$945{,}111{,}233 \div 250{,}000{,}000 \approx \$3.78$ per person (or, $\$945{,}111{,}233 \div 260{,}000{,}000 \approx \$3.64$ per person)

8b. $\$3.78 \times 365 \approx \$1380$ per person per year (or, $\$3.64 \times 365 \approx \$1329$ per person per year)

Connections

9. 70 million $\times 3 = 210$ million cigarettes

10. 3 million × 18 = 54 million cigarettes

11a. See below right.

11b. *Haiti:* six million, four hundred thousand; *People's Republic of China:* one billion, one hundred sixty-five million, eight hundred thousand

11c. *Haiti:* twenty-seven thousand, seven hundred thirty-nine; *Russia:* seventeen million, seventy-five thousand, three hundred fifty-two

11d. Answers will vary; look for reasonable explanations.

11e. In order by population density (numbers given in people per km^2): India (268), Haiti (231), People's Republic of China (121), France (104), Nigeria (98), United States (27), Brazil (18), Russia (8.7), Canada (2.7)

10. Health researchers estimate that 3 million Americans under age 18 smoke on a daily basis, averaging about 18 cigarettes per smoker per day. How many cigarettes are smoked by Americans under the age of 18 each day in the United States?

11. The table below gives the population and land area in 1992 for nine countries.

Country	Estimated population	Land area (km^2)
Brazil	150,800,000	8,511,957
Canada	27,400,000	9,976,136
France	56,900,000	547,033
Haiti	6,400,000	27,739
India	882,600,000	3,287,591
Nigeria	90,100,000	923,775
People's Republic of China	1,165,800,000	9,596,960
Russia	149,300,000	17,075,352
United States	255,600,000	9,363,109

Source: *1992 World Population Data Sheet* of the Population Reference Bureau, Inc.

a. Write each number in the table in scientific notation.

b. Write the numbers for the least and greatest populations in words.

c. Write the numbers for the least and greatest land areas in words.

d. When comparing two numbers, is it most useful to write the numbers in standard notation, scientific notation, or words? Explain your answer.

e. Divide each population by the corresponding land area to get the population per square kilometer. Then, order the countries by these population densities.

11a.

Country	Estimated population	Land area (km^2)
Brazil	1.508×10^8	8.511957×10^6
Canada	2.74×10^7	9.976136×10^6
France	5.69×10^7	5.47033×10^5
Haiti	6.4×10^6	2.7739×10^4
India	8.826×10^8	3.287591×10^6
Nigeria	9.01×10^7	9.23775×10^5
People's Republic of China	1.1658×10^9	9.59696×10^6
Russia	1.493×10^8	1.7075352×10^7
United States	2.556×10^8	9.363109×10^6

Extensions

12. Try to guess which state in the United States has the greatest population density and which state has the least population density. Then, look up population and land area data in an atlas or other source to check your guesses.

13. If you know the population density and land area for a country, state, or city, how can you calculate the population?

In 14–16, tell why the given conclusion is misleading, and explain how you could arrive at a better conclusion.

14. On an average day, about 300 Japanese students and about 900 American students drop out of school. *Misleading conclusion:* American students are three times more likely to drop out of school than Japanese students are.

15. On an average day, Japanese people make 200 million telephone calls, and Americans make 1800 million calls. *Misleading conclusion:* Americans make about nine times more phone calls each day than do Japanese.

16. On an average day, 10,726,000 Japanese travel by subway, and 6,323,000 Americans travel by subway. *Misleading conclusion:* About 1.7 times more Japanese travel by subway than do Americans.

Extensions

12. Based on 1996 data, New Jersey has the greatest population density, about 1065.4 people per square mile, and Alaska has the least, about 1.1 people per square mile. (Students may mention the District of Columbia, which has a population density of about 9347.1 people per square mile.)

13. If you know the population density and land area, you can calculate the population by multiplying the density by the area. For example, if the population density of Honolulu, Hawaii, is 4330 people per square mile and its land area is 85.7 square miles, the population is $4330 \times 85.7 \approx 371{,}100$ people.

14. The conclusion is misleading because it does not account for how many students there actually are in each country. It would be better to compare the ratios of dropouts to total number of students.

15. The conclusion is misleading because it does not account for the population of each country. It would be better to compare the ratios of calls made to the total population.

16. The conclusion is misleading because it does not account for the population of each country. It would be better to compare the ratios of the number of people who travel by subway to the total population.

17a. *Galileo* traveled from October 18, 1989, to December 7, 1995. This is 6 years and 50 days, plus one day for the leap year 1992, or 2241 days. This means that the probe traveled at a rate of 2,300,000,000,000 ÷ 2241 ≈ 1.03×10^9 miles per day, which is 1.03×10^9 miles/day ÷ 24 hours/day ≈ 43 million miles per hour.

17b. Radio signals travel at about 400,000,000 ÷ 50 = 8,000,000 miles per minute, so it would take about 1.9×10^{15} ÷ 8,000,000 = 2.38×10^8 minutes, or about 452 years, for them to travel this distance.

17c. Possible answer: Earth's diameter is 88,000 ÷ 11 ≈ 8000 miles, so Jupiter's diameter is about 80,000 miles greater than Earth's. It takes Jupiter 12 times as long as it takes Earth to travel around the sun. Assuming that the planets are spheres, Jupiter's circumference is 11 times Earth's circumference.

17d. no; An object's mass is related to its volume, while diameter is a linear measure. The mass of Jupiter might be close to 11^3 times that of Earth, depending on the composition of the planets.

17. Use the following newspaper article to answer a–d.

PROBE REACHES JUPITER FOR FIRST CLOSE-UP CONTACT WITH PLANET

After traveling over six years and more than 2,300,000,000,000 miles through space on a data-gathering mission, the *Galileo* spacecraft finally arrived at the planet Jupiter on December 7, 1995. The craft was released from the space shuttle *Atlantis* on October 18, 1989.

A space probe released from *Galileo* on July 13, 1995, slowed from its speed of 106,000 miles per hour as it entered Jupiter's atmosphere, beaming data to the waiting *Galileo* orbiting 133,000 miles above. The spacecraft relayed this infor-mation back to Earth, where scientists received the transmissions roughly 50 minutes after they were sent—the amount of time it takes radio signals to travel the 400,000,000 miles between Jupiter and our planet.

The largest planet in our solar system, Jupiter has a diameter of 88,000 miles, roughly 11 times that of Earth. An average distance of a half a billion miles from the sun, Jupiter takes almost 12 Earth years to make one complete circuit around the sun.

The mass of Earth is 600,588,000,000,000,000,000,000 short tons. This mass is read as 600 sextillion, 588 quintillion short tons. One short ton is 2000 pounds. ■

a. Find the average number of miles per day traveled by the *Galileo* spacecraft. How many miles per hour is this?

b. At what rate do radio signals travel between Jupiter and Earth? At this rate, how long would it take to send a signal to a spacecraft 1.9×10^{15} miles away?

c. Write some statements comparing Earth to Jupiter using information from this article.

d. Do you think that Jupiter's mass is 11 times Earth's mass? Why?

Mathematical Reflections

In this investigation, you continued to study data given as totals and as rates. You used ideas from *Comparing and Scaling* to make meaningful comparisons between the United States and Japan. These questions will help you summarize what you have learned:

1. Look back at your work from this and other investigations. Describe the methods you used to compare two or more numbers.

2. In a school fund-raiser, students at Hilltop Middle School sold calendars to their friends and families.

   a. Sales for the sixth grade were $500, sales for the seventh grade were $625, and sales for the eighth grade were $1000. If you were to write a story about the sale for the school paper, what comparison statements could you make on the basis of these data?

   b. At Hilltop, there are 100 sixth graders, 125 seventh graders, and 100 eighth graders. How would you adjust your statements from part a on the basis of this information?

3. How do you decide which method for comparing data is best in a given situation?

Think about your answers to these questions, discuss your ideas with other students and your teacher, and then write a summary of your findings in your journal.

Possible Answers

1. Two numbers can be compared by saying which is greater; by saying that one is greater by a specific amount (finding the difference); by saying that one is a certain number of times as great as the other (dividing the greater by the smaller); or by comparing the rates that produced the numbers.

2a. The eighth grade sold twice as much as the sixth grade. The seventh grade sold 1.25 times as much as the sixth grade. The sixth grade sold $125 less than the seventh grade and $500 less than the eighth grade.

2b. The eighth graders, on the average, sold twice as much as the sixth graders sold ($10 each as opposed to $5 each). The seventh graders sold, on the average, the same amount as the sixth graders sold ($5 each). The sixth graders sold, on the average, $5 less than the eighth graders sold.

3. See page 70.

Tips for the Linguistically Diverse Classroom

Original Rebus The Original Rebus technique is described in detail in *Getting to Know Connected Mathematics*. Students make a copy of the text before it is discussed. During the discussion, they generate their own rebuses for words they do not understand; the words are made comprehensible through pictures, objects, or demonstrations. Example: Question 2—Key phrases for which students might make rebuses are *school fund-raiser* (outline of a school labeled $), *calendars* (calendar page from current month), *write* (pencil), *school paper* (newspaper with school's name on it), *comparison statements* (2×, <, >).

TEACHING THE INVESTIGATION

6.1 • Recycling Cans

In this problem, students use addition and subtraction to derive information about recycling in Japan and the United States. In the follow-up, they use a benchmark to help them make sense of the great number of aluminum cans used in Japan.

Launch

To engage students in the topic of the recycling of aluminum cans, you might ask them to think back to the estimates they made in Problem 5.2 about the number of soft drink cans used in the United States. Then, ask that they make guesses about the number of aluminum cans that are and are not recycled every day in Japan and the United States, and to explain the thinking behind their guesses. You might also ask, based on their estimation, about how tall they think a stack of all the cans used in Japan or the United States on one day would be.

Once students are interested in the topic, read the problem with them. Make sure students recognize that these data were collected when the population of the United States was 250,000,000. This is a good time to discuss the fact that sources often differ in the data they report; when and how data are collected are two contributors to such differences.

Have students work individually or in pairs on the problem and follow-up.

Explore

This would be a good problem to have students do on their own, as you could then walk around and make individual assessments of their understanding of the concepts in this unit.

If students notice that the U.S. population figure given in this investigation does not equal that used in previous investigations, point out that the data in this investigation were collected at an earlier date.

Parts A and B are easy subtraction problems. Part C may cause some students difficulty because of the size of the number involved. As students find solutions to part C, be sure to ask them whether their answer is reasonable and why they think so.

Summarize

Have students share their answers to parts A and B.

> What operation did you use to get your answers?

Ask students to rewrite the answers to parts A and B using scientific notation. Expand on their work by asking these questions:

> How much greater is the number of cans recycled in the United States than the number recycled in Japan?
>
> Which form of notation—standard or scientific—is more convenient for making this comparison? Explain your answer.

Students may give different, but valid, answers; be sure they explain their reasoning. At this point, students will probably feel more comfortable with standard notation because they have not reasoned much about how to operate on numbers written in scientific notation. Many will say that using standard notation is easier because, to find the difference between two large numbers, the place-value positions may easily aligned.

Ask for the answers to part C, which requires students to multiply.

What operation did you use to get your answers?

The follow-up asks students to find the height of all the cans used in one day if they were stacked in a tower. Ask students to compare the height they find to some distance with which they are familiar. For example, 6247 kilometers is greater than the distance from Miami, Florida, to Seattle, Washington!

6.2 • Making Comparisons in Two Ways

The questions in this problem highlight two methods of comparing quantities, by using subtraction and by using division (or the idea of multiples).

Launch

Use the example in the student edition to introduce the problem, having students look at the two ways that the population figures might be compared. Ask them which comparison method they prefer and why. If they need more practice with these types of comparisons, offer another example.

When the class seems comfortable with the idea of making comparisons in the two ways demonstrated to emphasize different aspects about the quantities being compared, introduce the problem and the questions students are asked to answer. Have the class explore the problem and follow-up in groups of two or three.

Explore

Groups may want to divide the questions among the group members. If so, remind them that each person in the group should be comfortable with the group's answers. This means that the group must review each person's work, understand how the solutions were found, and resolve any disagreements they have.

Summarize

Call on different groups to explain their answer to each part of the problem, and then ask the class to add any other ideas they have.

For the Teacher: Discussing Differences Between Cultures

In discussing these and other comparisons between the United States and Japan, be careful about the raising of stereotypes. The differences in the cited statistics may reflect cultural variations, but they also reflect aspects of geography and population. For example, the population density of Japan is one of the reasons for the great use of public transportation in that country.

Once students have reviewed the problem, ask them to summarize their work by describing the two methods of comparison they used. A comparison based on finding differences between quantities is appropriate in some situations because the actual amount will be determined. However, finding how many times as great one quantity is compared to another is a powerful way to make comparisons because it shows the relationship between the amounts and often gives a better picture as to how the two amounts compare. Be sure students raise each of these techniques—subtraction and division—as well as variations that they think are important.

Ask for students' ideas about the follow-up.

6.3 • Comparing by Using Rates

This problem highlights the idea that comparisons of absolute quantities are often less meaningful than comparisons of rates. Students explored the concepts in this problem in detail in the *Comparing and Scaling* unit. Now, the size of the numbers adds a new complexity. This problem gives you an opportunity to review strategies for comparing data, to discuss similarities and differences among the various strategies, and to explore with students which type of comparison is most appropriate in a given situation.

Launch

Pose the question asked in the problem introduction, perhaps requesting that students keep their math books closed until the end of the launch.

Japanese take 714,500,000 pictures every month, and Americans take 1,250,200,000 pictures every month. What conclusions can you draw from this statement?

Knowing the populations of the two countries, what might you say about the number of pictures taken by Japanese compared to the number taken by Americans?

If there are 123,000,000 people in Japan, what is the average number of pictures taken per person per month? How did you find your answer?

If there are 250,000,000 people in the United States, what is the average number of pictures taken per person per month? How did you find your answer?

How do the averages—pictures per person in the United States and in Japan—compare?

How does comparing the average number of pictures taken per person change the way you think about the number of pictures people take?

Read Problem 6.3 with the class. Explain that they are to compare the sets of data in as many ways as they can. Remind them that they used two types of comparisons in Problem 6.2 and that you just discussed another type of comparison when you looked at the data about picture-taking.

Have students work in pairs on the problem and follow-up.

Explore

If students are not finding rates (per-person data) and using them, point this out and ask how they might use this type of comparison for working with the data in parts A and B.

Summarize

Have students share their answers, making sure they identify what operations they are using to make each comparison. Students will likely offer several opinions on the best type of comparison, such as the following:

- Some students may argue for using the difference comparison to analyze the number of smokers in the two countries.
- Some students, citing the great difference between the two population figures, may argue for a rate, or ratio, comparison for analyzing the number of smokers.
- Some students may propose using a factor to compare the number of smokers. For example, the number of smokers in the United States is about 1.7 times the number of smokers in Japan.

Be sure students talk about the strengths and weaknesses of each comparison.

The follow-up question may have been answered in the process of discussing the problem. Students might look at these figures and reach different conclusions about which country has more smoking. Students may say that the United States has 22 million more smokers and therefore the worse problem. A more informative comparison is the percent of smokers in each country: $\frac{55}{250}$ million, or 22%, of the U.S. population smokes, whereas $\frac{33}{123}$ million, or 27%, of Japan's population smokes. If students do not bring up this comparison, mention it yourself.

Another comparison is the number of cigarettes each smoker smokes per day. U.S. smokers smoke 26.1 cigarettes per day, whereas Japanese smokers smoke 25.7 cigarettes per day. These numbers are very close.

What should come out of this conversion is the idea that you can't just look at the difference in the number of people smoking and get a very good picture of the situation. More comparisons are needed for an accurate portrayal of the data.

Additional Answers

Answers to Problem 6.2

C. On an average day, Japanese children spend 1 hour 35 minutes longer in school than do American children. Or, Japanese children spend about 1.3 times as many hours in school as do American children. Or, American children spend about $\frac{3}{4}$ as many hours in school as do Japanese children.

E. On an average day, the percentage of Japanese using public transportation is 36 percentage points greater than the percentage of Americans using public transportation. (Note: This difference is tricky to discuss. You may need to help students express this idea.) Or, the percent of Japanese using public transportation on an average day is ten times the percent of Americans using it.

Answers to Problem 6.3

B. Possible answer: The number of cigarettes smoked on a typical day in the United States is 588 million greater than the number smoked on a typical day in Japan. There are 1,437,315,000 ÷ 849,315,000 = 1.7 times as many cigarettes smoked each day in the United States as are smoked in Japan. Also, 5.75 cigarettes per person are smoked per day in the United States, while 6.91 per person are smoked per day in Japan. The cigarettes-per-smoker-per-day rates are 26.1 in the United States and 25.7 in Japan, which is the best comparison because it shows how very similar the countries are in this respect.

Mathematical Reflections

3. To decide which method of comparison to use, you must take the purpose of the comparison and the types of data into account. If you have only total quantities, then differences make sense and tell one part of the story; finding what factor one quantity is of the other also makes sense and tells the relationship between the two numbers. If you have two measures for each situation, such as totals of cigarettes and people, rates often allow a more meaningful comparison.

Looking Back and Looking Ahead

Unit Reflections

The problems of this unit extended your understanding and skills in practical use of numbers and operations. You learned ways to *compare counts* and *measurements* in a variety of situations and how to work with very large and very small numbers. You developed skill in use of *place value* and *exponents* for *standard, scientific,* and *calculator number notation.*

Using Your Number Sense—To test your number sense, consider several important problem situations that require the ideas and strategies of numerical literacy.

1 *Here is a short newspaper report about flooding that occurred in parts of the midwestern United States in March of 1997. These eight numbers are missing:* 25; 60,000; 12; 26; 900; 38.8; 6; and 250,000,000.

> Record flooding has chased residents from their homes and killed __(1)__ people. Ninety-nine counties in __(2)__ states have been declared disaster areas following fierce weather that swept through the region. The Ohio River crested about __(3)__ feet above normal levels in Louisville, Kentucky. Normal river levels at this time of year are about __(4)__ feet, but Friday's high point was __(5)__ feet. Guardsmen built __(6)__-foot-long dikes using about __(7)__ sandbags. Officials estimate the waters have caused $__(8)__ in damage in Kentucky alone.

a. Match the missing numbers with the blanks in the story where you think they fit best.

b. Which numbers in the story do you think were estimates and which were probably determined from actual counts or measurements?

2 *According to the National Hurricane Center, from 1990–1996 there were 158 hurricanes. Hurricanes are categorized using the Saffir-Simpson Hurricane Scale, which gives a 1–5 rating based on the hurricane's intensity. Of the 158 storms,*

- *57 were category 1 (winds 74–95 mph with storm surge 3–5 feet above normal);*
- *37 were category 2 (winds 96–110 mph with storm surge 6–8 feet above normal);*

How to Use *Looking Back and Looking Ahead: Unit Reflections*

The first part of this section includes problems that allow students to demonstrate their mathematical understandings and skills. The second part gives them an opportunity to explain their reasoning. This section can be used as a review to help students stand back and reflect on the "big" ideas and connections in the unit. This section may be assigned as homework, followed up with class discussion the next day. Focus on the *Explaining Your Reasoning* section in the discussion. Encourage the students to refer to the problems to illustrate their reasoning.

Answers

Using Your Number Sense

1a. (1) 25 people – A smaller number makes sense given the type of disaster.

(2) 6 states

(3) 26 feet - This value added to 12 feet gives a sum close to the 38.8 feet high point.

(4) 12 feet

(5) 38.8 feet

(6) 900 foot - This value makes sense when tied to the 60,000 sandbags.

(7) 60,000 sandbags

(8) $250,000,000 in damage

b. The larger values (900, 60,000, and 250,000,000) are most likely estimates while the other values could have realistically come from counts or measurements.

- *47 were category 3 (winds 111–130 mph with storm surge 9–12 feet above normal);*
- *15 were category 4 (winds 131–155 mph with storm surge 13–18 feet above normal);*
- *2 were category 5 (winds greater than 155 mph with storm surge greater than 18 feet above normal).*

a. One equivalent measure is 1 mile ≈ 1.61 kilometers. For each of the five hurricane categories, write the ranges for wind speeds in km/h (kilometers per hour).

b. Another equivalent measure is 1 inch = 2.54 centimeters. For each of the five hurricane categories, write the ranges for storm surges in meters.

3 *Three of the most destructive hurricanes and the cost of damages each caused are listed.*

- *Andrew: 1992, category 4; $26,500,000,000*
- *Hugo: 1989, category 4; $7,000,000,000*
- *Fran: 1998, category 3; $3,200,000,000*

a. Write the cost of damages for each of the storms in scientific notation.

b. Compare the costs of the damages for the three storms in two ways and explain your choice for the better of the two comparison strategies.

i. by calculating the difference in costs for each pair

ii. by calculating the ratio of costs for each pair

c. Several numbers are used to measure the severity of hurricanes. Which numbers do you think are estimates and which are determined by actual measurements?

i. ranges of wind speeds

ii. ranges of storm surges

iii. costs for repair of storm damage

4 *The population in the United States includes people who are immigrants from many countries. The table on page 72 gives information about immigration by decade from 1901 to 1997.*

Possible Answers

Answers may vary due to rounding. Some students may use the upper limit for one category as the lower limit for the next and thus eliminate half the computations. Or, they may use one answer to find another. For example in part b, they may double, triple, ... the 3-ft surge to find 6-ft, 9-ft etc.

2a. Category 1 has winds 119.1 to 153.0 km/h.

Category 2 has winds 154.6 to 177.1 km/h.

Category 3 has winds 178.7 to 209.3 km/h.

Category 4 has winds 210.9 to 249.6 km/h.

Category 5 has winds greater than 249.6 km/h.

b. This conversion involves several steps: convert feet to inches, multiply by the conversion factor of 2.54 to get centimeters, and then finally, divide by 100 to change to meters.

Category 1 has storm surges 0.91 to 1.52 meters.

Category 2 has storm surges 1.83 to 2.44 meters.

Category 3 has storm surges 2.74 to 3.66 meters.

Category 4 has storm surges 3.96 to 5.49 meters.

Category 5 has storm surges above 5.49 meters.

3a. Andrew: $\$2.65 \times 10^{10}$

Hugo: $\$7 \times 10^{9}$

Fran: $\$3.2 \times 10^{9}$

b.

Storm Pair	**i.** Difference in Cost ($)	**ii.** Ratio of Costs
Andrew-Hugo	19,500,000	3.79
Andrew-Fran	23,300,000	8.28
Hugo-Andrew	–19,500,000	0.26
Hugo-Fran	3,800,000	2.19
Fran-Andrew	–23,300,000	0.12
Fran-Hugo	–3,800,000	0.46

The ratio comparison is better because it indicates how much more destructive Andrew was compared to Hugo and Fran—about 4 times and 8 times more, respectively. Or, the difference comparison is better because it highlights the monetary cost of Andrew.

c. **i.** measures, although not always exact **ii.** measures **iii.** estimates

U.S. Immigration: 1901–1997		
Period in Years	*Number in thousands*	*Rate per 1000 U.S. Population*
1901–1910	8795	10.4
1911–1920	5736	5.7
1921–1930	4107	3.5
1931–1940	528	0.4
1941–1950	1035	0.7
1951–1960	2515	1.5
1961–1970	3322	1.7
1971–1980	4493	2.1
1981–1990	7338	3.1
1991–1997	6945	3.8

Source: Statistical Abstract of the United States 1999 (page 10)

a. Write the number of people who immigrated during each period in standard notation.

b. Write each number of immigrants in scientific notation.

c. Which data would you suggest for ordering the decades for which immigration records are available from greatest to least: (1) the number in thousands; or (2) the rate per 1000 U.S. population?

Explaining Your Reasoning—Making sense of the numbers that occur in real-life problems requires careful reasoning. You need to be able to justify the use of estimates and exact counts or measurements, notation for large and small numbers, and strategies for comparing numbers.

1. How do you decide when a number reported in a story is an estimate and when it must be an exact count or measurement?

2. What is the value of using scientific notation? Explain, with illustrative examples, the procedures for using scientific notation to write very large numbers.

3. Very large numbers are often rounded in order to make them easier to read. Explain, with illustrative examples, general procedures for rounding

a. numbers that are greater than a million to the nearest thousand.

b. numbers that are greater than a billion to the nearest million.

4. Give examples that illustrate situations when it makes sense to compare two measurements or counts by finding

a. the difference of the two numbers.

b. the ratio of the two numbers.

4c. Either could be used.

The raw numbers can be misleading if they are not compared with the total U.S. population at the time. For example, while the 1980s had a larger number of immigrants than the 1910s, the rate per 1000 population in the 1910s was much greater than that of the 1980s.

Explaining Your Reasoning
See page 70d.

4.

Period in Years	**a.** Number in Standard Notation	**b.** Number in Scientific Notation
1901–1910	8,795,000	8.795×10^6
1911–1920	5,736,000	5.736×10^6
1921–1930	4,107,000	4.107×10^6
1931–1940	528,000	5.28×10^5
1941–1950	1,035,000	1.035×10^6
1951–1960	2,515,000	2.515×10^6
1961–1970	3,322,000	3.322×10^6
1971–1980	4,493,000	4.493×10^6
1981–1990	7,338,000	7.338×10^6
1991–1997	6,945,000	6.945×10^6

Looking Back and Looking Ahead

Possible Answers

Explaining Your Reasoning

1. One indication that the value is an estimate is the number of zeros it has. Very large numbers generally tend to be estimates. Key words such as "about," "almost," "around," and "nearly" are also indicators of estimates. Countable quantities are likely to be reported as exact values, as are measurable qualities such as temperature and speed.

2. Large numbers can be written using minimal space, and size comparisons can be done quickly by eliminating the need to count place values. To write 250,000,000 in scientific notation, start by placing a decimal point such that it makes a number that is at least 1 and less than 10. In this case, we would have 2.5. We need to multiply 2.5 by 100,000,000 in order to have 250,000,000. Since 100,000,000 can be written as 10^8, $250{,}000{,}000 = 2.5 \times 100{,}000{,}000$ or 2.5×10^8.

3a. To round a number to the nearest thousand, look at the hundreds digit. If the hundreds digit is 5 or greater, increase the number of thousands by 1. The hundreds digit and all digits to its right are replaced with zeros; the rounded number ends with three zeros to indicate we have rounded it to thousands. For example, to round 32,543,600 to the nearest thousand, start by noticing we have 6 hundreds. This is closer to the next thousand, so we adjust 3 thousand by adding 1 thousand to make it 4 thousand. So, 32,543,600 rounded to the nearest thousand is 32,544,000. Note the number of zeros is not always indicative of the rounding place. For example, 123,972 rounded to the nearest hundred or to the nearest thousand is the same number, 124,000.

b. To round a number to the nearest million, look at the hundred thousands digit. If this digit is 5 or greater, increase the number of millions by 1. The rounded number ends with six zeros to indicate we have rounded it. For example, to round 2,332,543,600 to the nearest million, start by noticing we have 5 hundred thousands (actually, more than 500,000). This is closer to the next million, so we adjust 2 million by adding 1 million to make it 3 million. The rounded answer is 2,333,000,000.

4a. When two values come from the same base (for example, population or group), we can compare their differences meaningfully. For example, we can meaningfully examine the difference between the number of girls in class A and the number of boys in class A.

b. Ratio comparisons make sense when comparing values that come from different sized bases (for example, different-sized populations or groups). Suppose we want to compare the number of girls in class A with the number of girls in class B. If the two classes have different total numbers of students, we cannot meaningfully compare the number of girls in class A with number of girls in class B. However, we could accurately compare the ratio of girls in class A to the ratio of girls in class B. Ratios may be used to compare the magnitudes of large numbers such as those in Problem 3.

Assessment Resources

Preparation Notes

Students will need calculators for all assessment pieces.

For the quiz, students will need to know the measurements of a school locker in customary units and approximately how many lockers are in the school. You may want to have them make the necessary measurements before starting the quiz, perhaps assigning the task of counting the lockers in the school to a small team of students, or checking with the school secretary.

Name ______________________ Date ____________

Check-Up

1. Write the customary unit of measure and the metric unit of measure that would be most reasonable for describing each item below.

	Customary unit	Metric unit
The perimeter of your school building		
The volume of your bathtub		
The height of a mouse		
The area of your state		
The volume of a shoe box		

2. The largest hotel in the world is in Las Vegas. The hotel cost $290 million to build and is on a 117-acre site. The Excalibur has 4032 deluxe rooms and employs a staff of 4000.*

   a. Which numbers are probably accurate, and which are probably rough estimates? For each number, explain your answer.

   b. Use the school's student population, its teacher population, or some other benchmark related to the school to make a statement about the size of the hotel staff.

3. It is estimated that the muscles in the human eye move 100,000 times or more each day.*

   a. About how many times do your eye muscles move in one year?

   b. Write your answer to part a in words.

   c. About how many movements do your eye muscles make in one second?

   d. About how many days will it take for your eye muscles to make one million movements?

*_Guinness Book of Records 1993._ Ed. Peter Matthews. New York: Bantam Books, 1993.

Names ______________________ Date ______________

Quiz

1. In one day Americans feed vending machines more than 250 million coins. All together, the coins are worth $34,000,000 and would occupy 8680 cubic feet.*

   a. To help you think about how much this is, find how many cubic feet of space is in your school locker.

   b. How many lockers would it take to hold the coins from one day of vending-machine operation?

   c. How many lockers are in your school? Could they hold all the coins from one day's vending-machine take? Explain.

   d. How many schools with the same number of lockers as yours would it take to hold the coins generated in *one year* from these vending machines?

2. In 1993, the U.S. national debt was $4,351,416,000,000, and the median household income was $31,241.

   a. If every household earned the median income and gave it all to the government to pay off the national debt, how many households would it take to pay the debt?

   b. Write your answer to part a in words.

   c. The world's highest paid executive in 1991 was Anthony O'Reilly, the CEO of Heinz. He made $75,085,000 in salary, stock options, and bonuses that year. How many of O'Reilly's yearly incomes would it take to pay off the 1993 U.S. national debt?

   d. Compare the 1993 median household income to O'Reilly's 1991 income in three different ways.

*Source: Tom Parker. *In One Day.* Boston: Houghton Mifflin, 1984.

Question Bank

Assign these questions as additional homework, or use them as review, quiz, or test questions.

In 1 and 2, refer to this report for two consecutive years on the hurricanes and tropical storms that reached the United States.*

Hurricanes and Tropical Storms

In 1992, the United States experienced seven hurricanes or tropical storms. There were 26 lives lost and $25,000,000,000 in property damage. In 1993, the United States experienced eight hurricanes or tropical storms. There were 9 lives lost and $57 million in property damage.

1. Which of the numbers in the reports are probably accurate, and which are probably rough estimates? Explain how you decided which numbers are accurate and which are estimates.

2. In a–c, make what you think is the best kind of comparison you can between the pair of events.

a. the number of hurricanes and tropical storms in 1992 and the number in 1993

b. the number of deaths due to hurricanes and tropical storms in 1992 and in 1993

c. the amount of property damage in 1992 and in 1993

3. In 1973, the average price for a gallon of regular leaded gasoline was 38.8¢. In 1983, the average price for a gallon of leaded gas was $1.157. This is a 198% increase in price.

a. If the price of leaded gas had continued to increase at the same rate for the next ten years, what would have been the average price for a gallon of leaded gas in 1993?

b. The last year leaded regular gas was sold in the United States was 1990. At that time, the average price per gallon was $1.149. Compared to the 1983 price, what percent change is this?

*Source: *Statistical Abstract of the United States 1995.* Published by the Bureau of the Census, Washington, D.C., p. 239.

In 4–9, use the information in the table, which shows the amount of spending on advertisement in several categories in 1994.

U.S. Ad Spending in 1994 (millions of dollars)

Category	Magazine	Newspaper	TV	Radio	Total
Automotive	1210.8	2521.4	4849.2	42.3	8988.1
Retail	210.1	4550.5	3101.2	126.6	8522.5
Business and consumer services	661.4	1562.2	3385.3	77.1	6518.6
Entertainment	76.1	691.1	3372.8	3.2	4388.1
Food	510.9	22.1	3190.0	44.4	3914.7
Toiletries and cosmetics	854.0	11.5	1898.6	15.1	2822.5
Drugs and remedies	432.8	104.0	1804.2	89.4	2561.2
Travel and hotels	436.7	891.3	622.6	18.5	2290.0

Source: Competitive Media Reporting and Publishers Information Bureau, as found in *The World Almanac and Book of Facts 1996.* Mahwah, N.J.: Funk and Wagnalls, 1995, p. 263.

4. Write the least number in the table in words.

5. Write the greatest number in the table in words.

6. After studying the numbers in the table, one could guess that they were rounded to the nearest hundred thousand dollars.

   a. If this is true, what is the greatest total amount, in dollars, that could have been spent on advertising by the retail industry in 1994?

   b. What is the least amount that could have been spent on advertising by the retail industry in 1994?

7. Rank the eight categories listed from greatest to least based on their spending for magazine ads.

8. For each of the eight categories listed, find the percent of the total advertising budget spent on TV ads.

9. Make three statements comparing the ways the food industry and the automotive industry spent money for advertising in 1994.

In 10–17, use this information: Sometimes you need to change from customary units of measure to metric units of measure or vice versa. Here are some common conversions:

1 inch = 2.54 centimeters	1 gallon = 3.785 liters
1 pound = 0.454 kilogram	1 mile = 1.61 kilometers

10. Joan is 5 feet 2 inches tall. Convert this to a convenient metric measurement.

11. Lendon weights 115 pounds. Convert this to a convenient metric measurement.

12. If a car holds 22 gallons of gas when its tank is full, how many liters will it hold?

13. The distance by air from New York to Los Angeles is about 2500 miles. How many kilometers is this?

14. Daniel, a professional basketball player, is 2 meters tall. Convert this to a convenient customary measurement.

15. Daniel has a mass of 90 kilograms. Convert this to a convenient customary measurement.

16. How many gallons does a 2-liter bottle hold? How many quarts does it hold?

17. The distance by air from Detroit to Miami is about 1850 kilometers. How many miles is this?

In 18–21, use the information in the table, which shows the amount of different types of paper currency in circulation in the United States.

U.S. Bills in Circulation

Denomination	Total dollar amount in circulation
$1	$5,845,268,648
$2	1,003,940,584
$5	6,948,740,110
$10	13,013,456,290
$20	76,265,781,080
$50	42,906,224,700

Source: Financial Management Service, U.S. Dept. of the Treasury, as found in *The World Almanac and Book of Facts 1996.* Mahwah, N.J.: Funk and Wagnalls, 1995, p. 121.

18. In words, write the total dollar amount of the $1 denomination in circulation.

19. In words, write the total dollar amount of the $2 denomination in circulation.

20. Round each dollar amount in the table to an appropriate place value.

21. Write each number from your answer to question 19 in scientific notation.

Name ______________________ Date ____________

Unit Test

Be sure to show the numbers and the operations you use to find each solution.

On a typical day, the U.S. Mint stamps out 3.5 million quarters, 3,700,000 dimes, 3,000,000 nickels, and 39 million pennies.*

1. a. What is the value of one days' production of coins?

   b. If the mint mills run five days a week, how much money in coins would be produced in one year?

   c. Write your answer to part b in words.

   d. Write your answer to part b in scientific notation.

2. a. Given the U.S. population of about 260 million, how much money per person is produced in coins in one year?

   b. Round your answer to part a to an appropriate place value. Explain why you rounded the number as you did.

3. a. How many coins are produced by the U.S. Mint in one day?

   b. Write your answer to part a in words.

*Source: Tom Parker. *In One Day.* Boston: Houghton Mifflin, 1984.

Name ______________________________ Date ______________

Unit Test

c. How many coins are produced by the U.S. Mint in one year? Assume the mint operates five days a week.

4. A quarter is $\frac{1}{16}$ of an inch thick. If you could put all the quarters produced by the U.S. Mint in one day in a stack, how high would the stack be

a. in inches?

b. in feet?

c. in yards?

d. Compare the height of the stack of quarters with some familiar measure or personal benchmark of your own. State the relationship between the height of the stack of quarters and your benchmark.

5. Make three *different* kinds of comparisons about the number of coins (quarters, dimes, nickels, and/or pennies) produced, or about the value of the coins produced, in one day in the United States.

Name ______________________________ Date ____________

Notebook Checklist

Journal Organization

_____ Problems and Mathematical Reflections are labeled and dated.

_____ Work is neat and is easy to find and follow.

Vocabulary

_____ All words are listed. _____ All words are defined or described.

Check-Up and Quiz

_____ Check-Up _____ Quiz

Homework Assignments

_____ ______________________________

_____ ______________________________

_____ ______________________________

_____ ______________________________

_____ ______________________________

_____ ______________________________

_____ ______________________________

_____ ______________________________

_____ ______________________________

_____ ______________________________

_____ ______________________________

_____ ______________________________

_____ ______________________________

_____ ______________________________

_____ ______________________________

_____ ______________________________

Name ______________________________ Date ______________

Self-Assessment

Vocabulary

Of the vocabulary words I defined or described in my journal, the word ______________ best demonstrates my ability to give a clear definition or description.

Of the vocabulary words I defined or described in my journal, the word ______________ best demonstrates my ability to use an example to help explain or describe an idea.

Mathematical Ideas

Large numbers are used to describe a variety of situations.

1. a. After studying the mathematics in *Data Around Us,* I learned the following about making sense of large numbers, choosing sensible units for measuring, comparing counts and measures, reading and writing numbers, and estimating and rounding numbers:

b. Here are page numbers of journal entries that give evidence of what I have learned, along with descriptions of what each entry shows:

2. a. These are the mathematical ideas I am still struggling with:

b. This is why I think these ideas are difficult for me:

c. Here are page numbers of journal entries that give evidence of what I am struggling with, along with descriptions of what each entry shows:

Class Participation

I contributed to the class discussion and understanding of *Data Around Us* when I . . . (Give examples.)

Answers to the Check-Up

1. Possible answer:

	Customary unit	Metric unit
The perimeter of your school building	yards	meters
The volume of your bathtub	gallons	liters
The height of a mouse	inches	centimeters
The area of your state	square miles	square kilometers
The volume of a shoe box	cubic inches	cubic centimeters

2. **a.** The figure $290 million is probably an estimate rounded to the nearest million or ten million dollars; it is common to round very large numbers. The staff of 4000 is probably an estimate; it seems to be a rounded number, and an exact staff count would be hard to make because it probably changes often. The figures 117 acres and 4032 rooms both appear to be exact; both are given to the ones place (although the land might be rounded to the nearest acre) and are probably constant, and it would be easy to count acres and numbers of rooms.

   b. Possible answers: Our school has about 540 students, so it would take approximately seven and a half schools of our size to staff the hotel. There are 25 teachers in our school; the hotel staff is 160 times greater than this.

3. **a.** $100{,}000 \times 365 = 36{,}500{,}000$ times

   b. thirty-six million, five hundred thousand

   c. $100{,}000 \div 24 \div 60 \div 60 \approx 1.16$ movements per second

   d. 10 days

Answers to the Quiz

1. **a.** Possible answer: A locker measuring 12 in by 13.5 in by 4 ft 9 in has $1 \text{ ft} \times 1.125 \text{ ft} \times 4.75 \text{ ft} \approx 5.34 \text{ ft}^3$ of space.

   b. $8680 \div 5.34 \approx 1630$ lockers

   c. Answers will vary. The school mentioned above has 475 lockers, so it could not hold all the coins from one day's vending-machine take.

   d. It would require $1630 \div 475 \approx 3.43$ schools of the size of the one mentioned above to hold one day's take, and $3.43 \times 365 \approx 1250$ schools to hold the coins generated in one year.

2. **a.** $4{,}351{,}416{,}000{,}000 \div 31{,}241 \approx 139{,}285{,}426$ households

   b. one hundred thirty-nine million, two hundred eighty-five thousand, four hundred twenty-six

   c. $4{,}351{,}416{,}000{,}000 \div 75{,}085{,}000 \approx 57{,}953$ of O'Reilly's incomes

   d. O'Reilly earned $75,053,759 more than the median income. O'Reilly's income was about 2400 times the median income. The median income was 0.042% of O'Reilly's income.

Answers to the Question Bank

1. The number of hurricanes and lives lost are probably accurate, because they are very small numbers, and people probably keep accurate records of these things. The amount of damage is probably an estimate, because it is a large amount, appears to be rounded, and would be difficult to assess exactly.

2. **a.** Possible answer: There was one more tropical storm or hurricane in 1993 than in 1992.

   b. Possible answer: The storms of 1992 caused about three times the number of deaths caused by the storms of 1993.

   c. Possible answer: The amount of property damage in 1992 was about 440 times that in 1993.

3. **a.** $\$1.157 + (\$1.157 \times 1.98) \approx \$3.448$ per gallon

   b. The price fell by about 1% from 1983 to 1990. The 1990 price is 99% of the 1983 price.

4. three million, two hundred thousand

5. eight billion, nine hundred eighty-eight million, one hundred thousand

6. **a.** $8,522,549,999

   b. $8,522,450,000

7. automotive, toiletries and cosmetics, business and consumer services, food, travel and hotels, drugs and remedies, retail, entertainment

8. automotive, about 54.0%; retail, about 36.4%; business and consumer services, about 51.9%; entertainment, about 76.9%; food, about 81.5%; toiletries and cosmetics, about 67.3%; drugs and remedies, about 70.4%; travel and hotels, about 27.2%

9. Possible answers: The automotive industry spent $5,073,400,000 more on advertising than did the food industry. The automotive industry spent 2.3 times on advertising than the food industry spent. The automotive industry spent about 114 times on newspaper advertising than the food industry spent. The automotive industry spent more than twice on magazine advertising as the food industry spent. The automotive industry spent about 54.0% of their advertising money on TV, while the food industry spent about 81.5% of their advertising money on TV.

10. $62 \times 2.54 \approx 157.48$ cm or 1.57 m

11. $115 \times 0.454 = 52.21$ kg

12. $22 \times 3.785 = 83.27$ l

13. $2500 \times 1.61 = 4025$ km

14. $200 \div 2.54 = 78.7$ in or about 6 ft 7 in

15. $90 \div 0.454 \approx 198$ lb

16. $2 \div 3.785 = 0.528$ gal, $0.528 \times 4 \approx 2.11$ qt

17. $1850 \div 1.61 \approx 1149$ mi

18. five billion, eight hundred forty-five million, two hundred sixty-eight thousand, six hundred forty-eight

19. one billion, three million, nine hundred forty thousand, five hundred eighty-four

20. Possible answer:

Denomination	Total dollar amount in circulation
$1	$5,800,000,000
$2	1,000,000,000
$5	6,900,000,000
$10	13,000,000,000
$20	76,300,000,000
$50	42,900,000,000

21. Possible answer:

Denomination	Total dollar amount in circulation
$1	$\$5.8 \times 10^9$
$2	1.0×10^9
$5	6.9×10^9
$10	1.3×10^{10}
$20	7.63×10^{10}
$50	4.29×10^{10}

Answers to the Unit Test

1. a. quarters: $3,500,000 \times 0.25 = \$875,000$
   dimes: $3,700,000 \times 0.10 = \$370,000$
   nickels: $3,000,000 \times 0.05 = \$150,000$
   pennies: $39,000,000 \times 0.01 = \$390,000$
   total: $1,785,000

   b. $\$1,785,000 \times 5 \times 52 = \$464,100,000$

   c. four hundred sixty-four million, one hundred thousand

   d. 4.641×10^8

2. a. $\$464,100,000 \div 260,000,000 = \$1.785$ per person per year

   b. $1.79; This is rounded to the nearest cent (one hundredth) because the amount is very small and this is a common way to write money amounts.

3. **a.**

quarters:	3,500,000
dimes:	3,700,000
nickels:	3,000,000
pennies:	39,000,000
total:	49,200,000 coins

b. forty-nine million, two hundred thousand

c. $49{,}200{,}000 \times 5 \times 52 = 12{,}792{,}000{,}000$ coins

4. **a.** $3{,}500{,}000 \div 16 = 218{,}750$ in

b. $218{,}750 \div 12 \approx 18{,}229$ ft

c. $18{,}229 \div 3 \approx 6076$ yd

d. Possible answers: The length of a football field, including end zones, is 120 yards, so the stack of quarters is about $6076 \div 120 = 50.6$ football fields tall. The length of a football field from goal line to goal line is 100 yards, so the stack of quarters is about 60.8 fields tall.

5. Possible answer: The U.S. Mint produces 11 times as many pennies as quarters every day. About 7% of the coins produced each day are quarters. About 79% of the coins produced each day are pennies. Quarters make up about 49%, or one half, of the value of the coins produced daily. About 200,000 more dimes than quarters are produced each day.

The final assessment for *Data Around Us* is a unit test. Below is a suggested scoring rubric and a grading scale for the unit test, followed by samples of student work and a teacher's comments on each sample.

Suggested Scoring Rubric

This rubric employs a scale with a total of 28 possible points. You may use the rubric as presented here or modify it to fit your district's requirements for evaluating and reporting students' work and understanding.

In the grading of the test, students are not penalized twice for an error. If a student derives a value that is incorrect, and then carries out a correct procedure using the incorrect value, he or she is given credit for the correct procedure. For example, if a student has an incorrect amount for question 1b and uses that amount in question 2a, points are not deducted for the incorrect answer that results from using that incorrect amount.

7 points (question 1)

Part a

- 3 points for a correct and labeled answer with enough written work for the reader to follow the student's thinking
- 2 points for an incorrect answer but work showing a correct strategy and appropriate reasoning ***or*** a correct answer but incomplete written work
- 1 point for an incorrect answer but some appropriate reasoning
- 0 points for an incorrect answer and no reasonable work

Part b

- 2 points for a correct and labeled answer with appropriate written work
- 1 point for an incorrect answer but work showing some correct reasoning ***or*** a correct answer but no written work
- 0 points for an incorrect answer and no reasonable work

Part c

- 1 point for a correct answer

Part d

- 1 point for a correct answer

5 points (question 2)

Part a

- 2 points for a correct and labeled answer with appropriate written work
- 1 point for an incorrect answer but work showing some correct reasoning ***or*** a correct answer but no written work
- 0 points for an incorrect answer and no reasonable work

Part b

- 3 points for a correct answer and a complete explanation
- 2 points for a correct answer and a partial or weak explanation
- 1 point for a correct answer but no explanation ***or*** an incorrect answer but some correct reasoning
- 0 points for an incorrect answer and no reasoning

5 points (question 3)

Part a

- 2 points for a correct and labeled answer with appropriate written work
- 1 point for an incorrect answer but work showing some correct reasoning ***or*** a correct answer but no written work
- 0 points for an incorrect answer and no reasonable work

Part b

- 1 point for a correct answer

Part c

- 2 points for a correct and labeled answer with appropriate written work
- 1 point for an incorrect answer but work showing some correct reasoning ***or*** a correct answer but no written work
- 0 points for an incorrect answer and no reasonable work

6 points (question 4)

Parts a, b, and c

- 1 point for each correct answer ***and*** 1 additional point for using a reasonable strategy (all three parts can be solved using the same strategy, such as division, though calculations might be incorrect)

Part d

- 2 points for selecting a reasonable benchmark and using it correctly
- 1 point for selecting a weak benchmark but using it correctly ***or*** making an incorrect comparison
- 0 points for using the benchmark incorrectly

5 points (question 5)

- 1 point for each correct comparison (3 points possible) ***and*** 1 point for each statement that is a different kind of comparison than the first one given (2 points possible)

Grading Scale

Points	*Grade*
25 to 28	A
21 to 24	B
17 to 20	C
14 to 16	D

Sample 1

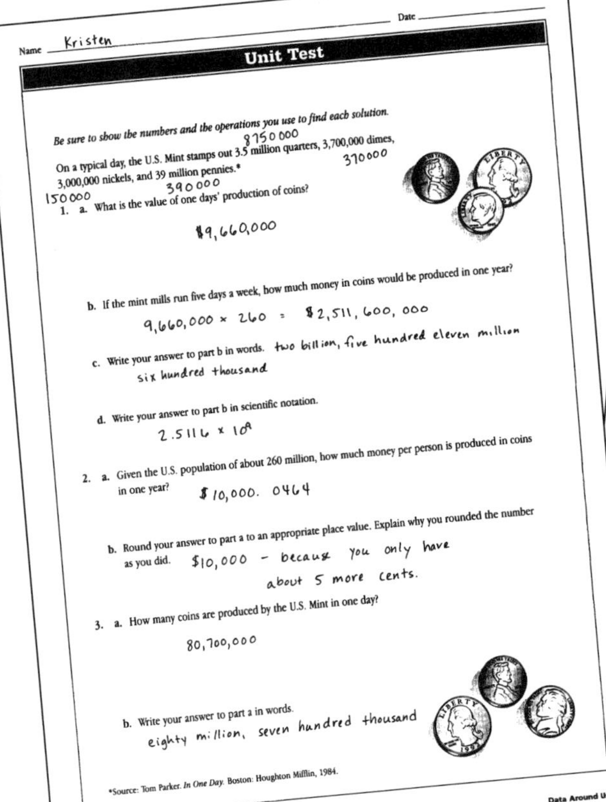
Name Kristen   Date

Unit Test

Be sure to show the numbers and the operations you use to find each solution.

On a typical day, the U.S. Mint stamps out 3.5 million quarters, 3,700,000 dimes, 3,000,000 nickels, and 39 million pennies.*

875 0 000   370000
150000   390 000

1. a. What is the value of one days' production of coins?

$9,660,000

b. If the mint mills run five days a week, how much money in coins would be produced in one year?

9,660,000 × 260 = $2,511,600,000

c. Write your answer to part b in words. two billion, five hundred eleven million six hundred thousand

d. Write your answer to part b in scientific notation.

2.5116 × 10^9

2. a. Given the U.S. population of about 260 million, how much money per person is produced in coins in one year? $10,000. 0464

b. Round your answer to part a to an appropriate place value. Explain why you rounded the number as you did. $10,000 - becaus you only have about 5 more cents.

3. a. How many coins are produced by the U.S. Mint in one day?

80,700,000

b. Write your answer to part a in words.

eighty million, seven hundred thousand

*Source: Tom Parker. *In One Day*. Boston: Houghton Mifflin, 1984.

78 Assessment Resources   Data Around Us

Name Kristen   Date

Unit Test

c. How many coins are produced by the U.S. Mint in one year? Assume the mint operates five days a week.

20,982,000,000

4. A quarter is $\frac{1}{16}$ of an inch thick. If you could put all the quarters produced by the U.S. Mint in one day in a stack, how high would the stack be   3.5 million ÷ 16

a. in inches?

21 875 00 inches tall
÷ 12 =

b. in feet?

182291.67 ft tall
÷ 3 =

c. in yards?

6076. 3889 yrds tall

d. Compare the height of the stack of quarters with some familiar measure or personal benchmark of your own. State the relationship between the height of the stack of quarters and your benchmark.

60.76 3889 football fields long

5. Make three *different* kinds of comparisons about the number of coins (quarters, dimes, nickels, and/or pennies) produced, or about the value of the coins produced, in one day in the United States.

* there are 500p00 more quarters made than nickles made in a day
* ther are 200,000 more dimes made than quarters
* there are 38700000 more pennies made than

35,000,000
35 00000
37000000

Data Around Us

Assessment Resources 79

Teacher's Comments on Rex's Unit Test

Rex earned 18.5 of the 28 possible points. For question 1, part a he correctly finds the value of one day's production of coins and gives supporting work, thus receiving 3 points. For part b, he finds the correct amount of money produced in one year but does not show how he arrives at his answer, thus earning 1 point instead of 2. For parts c and d, he received full credit.

Rex received no points for question 2, part a. His answer is incorrect and, because he gives no evidence of how he computes it, I am unsure how he arrives at his number. I expect my students to use calculators but that does not excuse them from recording what they enter into the machine. I can't analyze mistakes and work to correct them if I am not aware of students' misconceptions. For part b, Rex received 2 of the 3 possible points, as his explanation is weak. It is not acceptable in my class to state the standard rounding rule incompletely. Rex was given credit for his answer because it is reasonable based on what he has for part a. Not giving credit for a correct rounding of what he had for part a would penalize him twice.

Rex earned only 3 of the 5 possible points for question 3. For question 4, he received 5 of the 6 possible points. For both questions, Rex lost points for not showing his work. I talk about this often to my students, but I am still having trouble getting them to address the issue. I am not going to change my rubric because I feel it is important that students show their thinking. I plan to talk more with others in the department and with the teachers in earlier grades and see whether this is a common concern; we might be able to brainstorm some ways to address it across the grade levels.

Rex's work for question 5 is weak. This is the second unit in which students have been asked to write comparisons, but none of Rex's answers are very mathematically powerful. Though they are technically correct, I have given him only half credit for his work. The norm in my class for what it means to make comparisons is higher than what is demonstrated on this paper.

His overall performance on the test indicates to me that Rex has made reasonable sense of the mathematics in this unit.

Sample 2

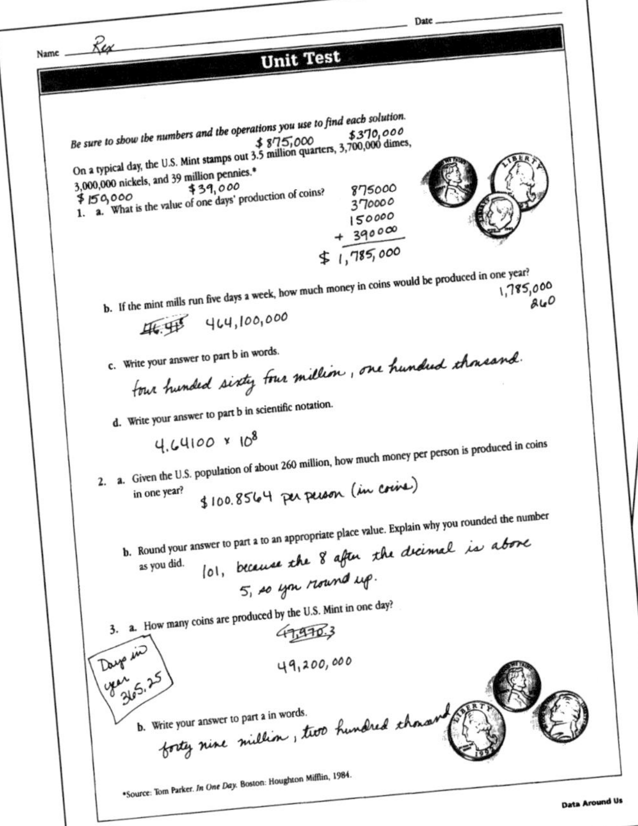
Name Rex Date

Unit Test

Be sure to show the numbers and the operations you use to find each solution.

On a typical day, the U.S. Mint stamps out 3.5 million quarters, 3,700,000 dimes, 3,000,000 nickels, and 39 million pennies.*

$875,000 $370,000 $150,000 $39,000

1. a. What is the value of one days' production of coins?

875000
370000
150000
+ 390000
$1,785,000

b. If the mint mills run five days a week, how much money in coins would be produced in one year?

1,785,000
260
464,100,000

c. Write your answer to part b in words.

four hundred sixty four million, one hundred thousand.

d. Write your answer to part b in scientific notation.

4.64100×10^8

2. a. Given the U.S. population of about 260 million, how much money per person is produced in coins in one year?

$100.8564 per person (in coins)

b. Round your answer to part a to an appropriate place value. Explain why you rounded the number as you did.

101, because the 8 after the decimal is above 5, so you round up.

3. a. How many coins are produced by the U.S. Mint in one day?

Days in year 365.25

49,200,000

b. Write your answer to part a in words.

forty nine million, two hundred thousand

*Source: Tom Parker. *In One Day.* Boston: Houghton Mifflin, 1984.

78 Assessment Resources Data Around Us

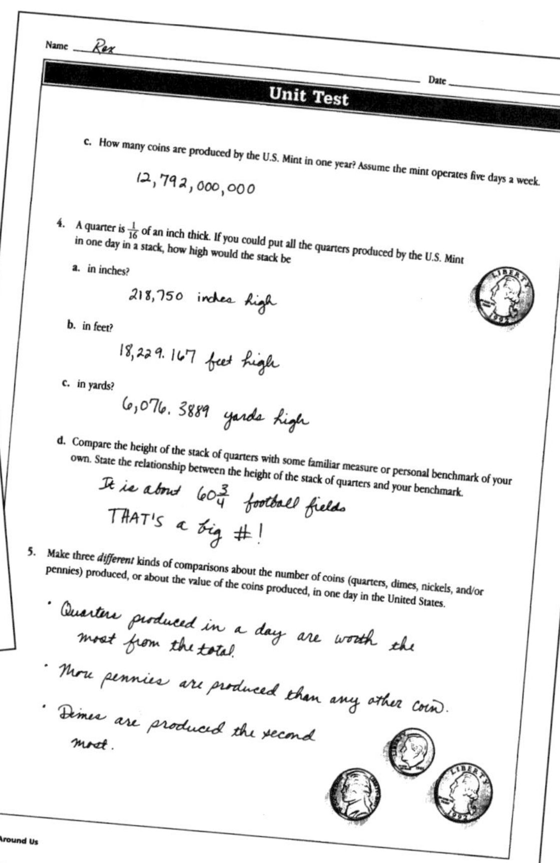
Name Rex Date

Unit Test

c. How many coins are produced by the U.S. Mint in one year? Assume the mint operates five days a week.

12,792,000,000

4. A quarter is $\frac{1}{16}$ of an inch thick. If you could put all the quarters produced by the U.S. Mint in one day in a stack, how high would the stack be

a. in inches?

218,750 inches high

b. in feet?

18,229.167 feet high

c. in yards?

6,076.3889 yards high

d. Compare the height of the stack of quarters with some familiar measure or personal benchmark of your own. State the relationship between the height of the stack of quarters and your benchmark.

It is about $60\frac{3}{4}$ football fields
THAT'S a big #!

5. Make three *different* kinds of comparisons about the number of coins (quarters, dimes, nickels, and/or pennies) produced, or about the value of the coins produced, in one day in the United States.

- Quarters produced in a day are worth the most from the total.
- More pennies are produced than any other coin.
- Dimes are produced the second most.

Data Around Us Assessment Resources 79

Teacher's Comments on Kristen's Unit Test

Kristen earned 17 points for her work on the test. For question 1, part a she earned only 1 point. Her answer shows some correct reasoning based on the values she has written above the coin counts. Close examination shows her error and why she has the incorrect answer: for the value of the quarters, she has written 8,750,000 instead of 875,000. This is not surprising because throughout the unit Kristen has experimented with large numbers. She has not always entered the complete number, leaving off zeros to the right of the other digits and adding them back after she has added or multiplied the truncated numbers. My guess is that when she was determining the value of the quarters, she multiplied 3.5×25 and then tried to figure out how many zeros were needed. This strategy is one that she has shared in class. Because she is still struggling with this idea, I need to talk to her about this strategy and try to help her become more efficient in using it. Kristen received all 4 points for parts b, c, and d, as her answers are correct based on her answer for part a. To take off points here would penalize her twice for her place-value error.

Kristen received no points for question 2, part a. Her answer is incorrect and she shows no work. Her answer is interesting in that if you were to remove three zeros you would have the correct number based on her other answers. That is, if you take 2,511,600,000 (her answer to question 1, part b) and divide it by 250 million, you get 10.0464; Kristen's answer is 10,000.0464. I think she is again trying to take away zeros and add them back in after working with a truncated number. She received 2 of the 3 points for part b because her explanation is weak for a second-semester seventh grader.

The answer Kristen gives for question 3, part a is a mystery to me, and no work is shown. Kristen is given 1 point for part b because it is correct based on her answer to part a. She received 1 point for part c because it is correct if you start with 80,700,000 and multiply it by 260 (the number of working days in a 52-week, 5-days-a-week schedule).

Kristen earned 5 of the 6 points for question 4. She has a correct strategy and correct solutions for parts a, b, and c. Her benchmark, a football field, is good, and her calculation is correct but the statement is unclear.

Kristen's work for question 5 is minimal. I gave her 3 points for her comparisons, which are all correct. I need to think about this question and either find a better way to word the request or work harder throughout the unit to help students make more sophisticated comparisons than just finding differences.

Kristen has grasped the basic ideas of the unit but, as stated above, we need to talk more about her strategy of dropping and adding zeros.

Blackline Masters

Labsheets

Transparencies

Additional Resources

Exxon Valdez Oil Spill

Shortly after **A** ____________ on **B** ____________ a giant oil tanker left Valdez, Alaska, with a load of **C** ____________ of crude oil from the Alaskan pipeline. To avoid icebergs, the ship took a course about **D** ____________ out of the normal shipping channel. Unfortunately, less than **E** ____________ later the ship ran aground on the underwater Bligh Reef. The rocks of the reef tore a **F** ____________ gash in the tanker's hull, and **G** ____________ of crude oil spilled onto the surface of Prince William Sound. For weeks, the world watched closely as the *Exxon Valdez* oil spill became an environmental disaster, despite extensive efforts to contain and clean up the oil. The spill gradually spread to form an oil slick, covering **H** ____________ of water and killing **I** ____________ sea otters and **J** ____________ birds. The cleanup engaged **K** ____________ of boats and workers, who struggled against the cold of **L** ____________ water and air temperatures. The cleanup cost was over **M** ____________, including **N** ____________ for wildlife rescue alone.

Match each lettered blank with the correct measurement or range of numbers from the list below. Be prepared to explain your reasons for each choice.

800 square miles	10,080,000 gallons	$41 million
2000 to 3000	600-foot	2 miles
40° Fahrenheit	150 centimeters	90,000 to 300,000
$2 billion	March 24, 1989	52,000,000 gallons
thousands	3 hours	9:00 P.M.

Spinners for Dialing Digits

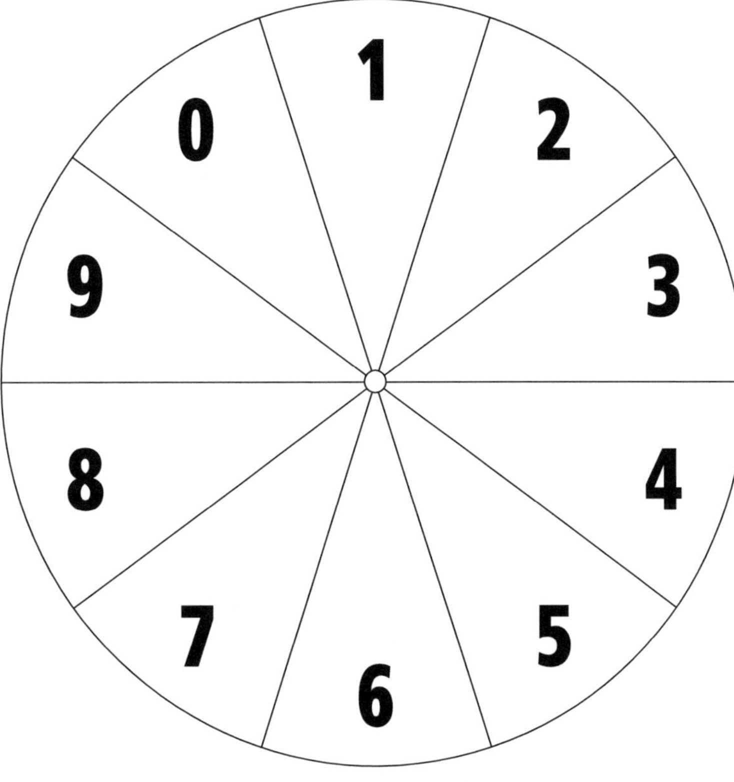

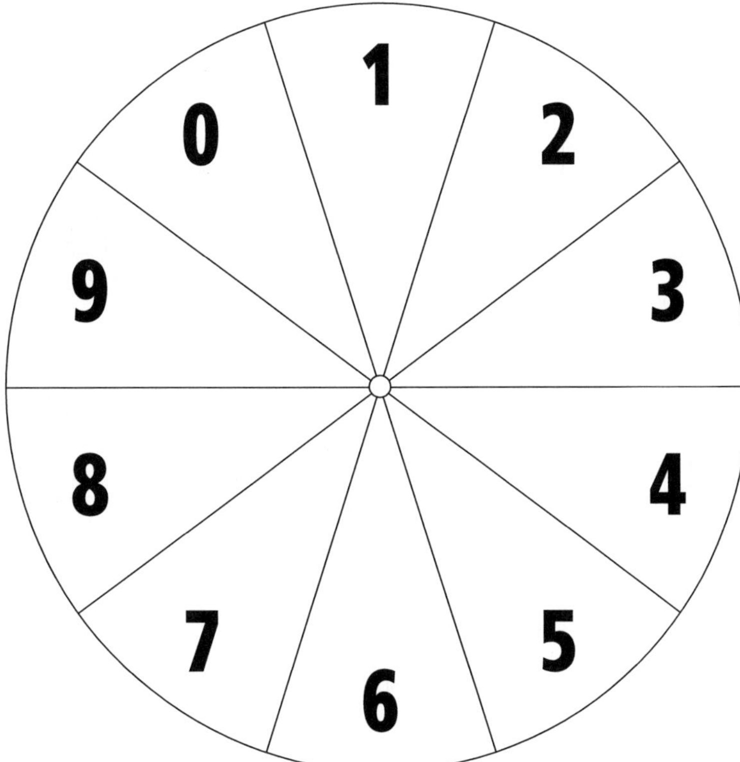

Game Cards for Dialing Digits

Dialing Digits	Dialing Digits
Game 1 ☐☐☐, ☐☐☐, ☐☐☐	Game 1 ☐☐☐, ☐☐☐, ☐☐☐
Game 2 ☐☐☐, ☐☐☐, ☐☐☐	Game 2 ☐☐☐, ☐☐☐, ☐☐☐
Game 3 ☐☐☐, ☐☐☐, ☐☐☐	Game 3 ☐☐☐, ☐☐☐, ☐☐☐
Game 4 ☐☐☐, ☐☐☐, ☐☐☐	Game 4 ☐☐☐, ☐☐☐, ☐☐☐
Dialing Digits	**Dialing Digits**
Game 1 ☐☐☐, ☐☐☐, ☐☐☐	Game 1 ☐☐☐, ☐☐☐, ☐☐☐
Game 2 ☐☐☐, ☐☐☐, ☐☐☐	Game 2 ☐☐☐, ☐☐☐, ☐☐☐
Game 3 ☐☐☐, ☐☐☐, ☐☐☐	Game 3 ☐☐☐, ☐☐☐, ☐☐☐
Game 4 ☐☐☐, ☐☐☐, ☐☐☐	Game 4 ☐☐☐, ☐☐☐, ☐☐☐
Dialing Digits	**Dialing Digits**
Game 1 ☐☐☐, ☐☐☐, ☐☐☐	Game 1 ☐☐☐, ☐☐☐, ☐☐☐
Game 2 ☐☐☐, ☐☐☐, ☐☐☐	Game 2 ☐☐☐, ☐☐☐, ☐☐☐
Game 3 ☐☐☐, ☐☐☐, ☐☐☐	Game 3 ☐☐☐, ☐☐☐, ☐☐☐
Game 4 ☐☐☐, ☐☐☐, ☐☐☐	Game 4 ☐☐☐, ☐☐☐, ☐☐☐
Dialing Digits	**Dialing Digits**
Game 1 ☐☐☐, ☐☐☐, ☐☐☐	Game 1 ☐☐☐, ☐☐☐, ☐☐☐
Game 2 ☐☐☐, ☐☐☐, ☐☐☐	Game 2 ☐☐☐, ☐☐☐, ☐☐☐
Game 3 ☐☐☐, ☐☐☐, ☐☐☐	Game 3 ☐☐☐, ☐☐☐, ☐☐☐
Game 4 ☐☐☐, ☐☐☐, ☐☐☐	Game 4 ☐☐☐, ☐☐☐, ☐☐☐

Map of the United States

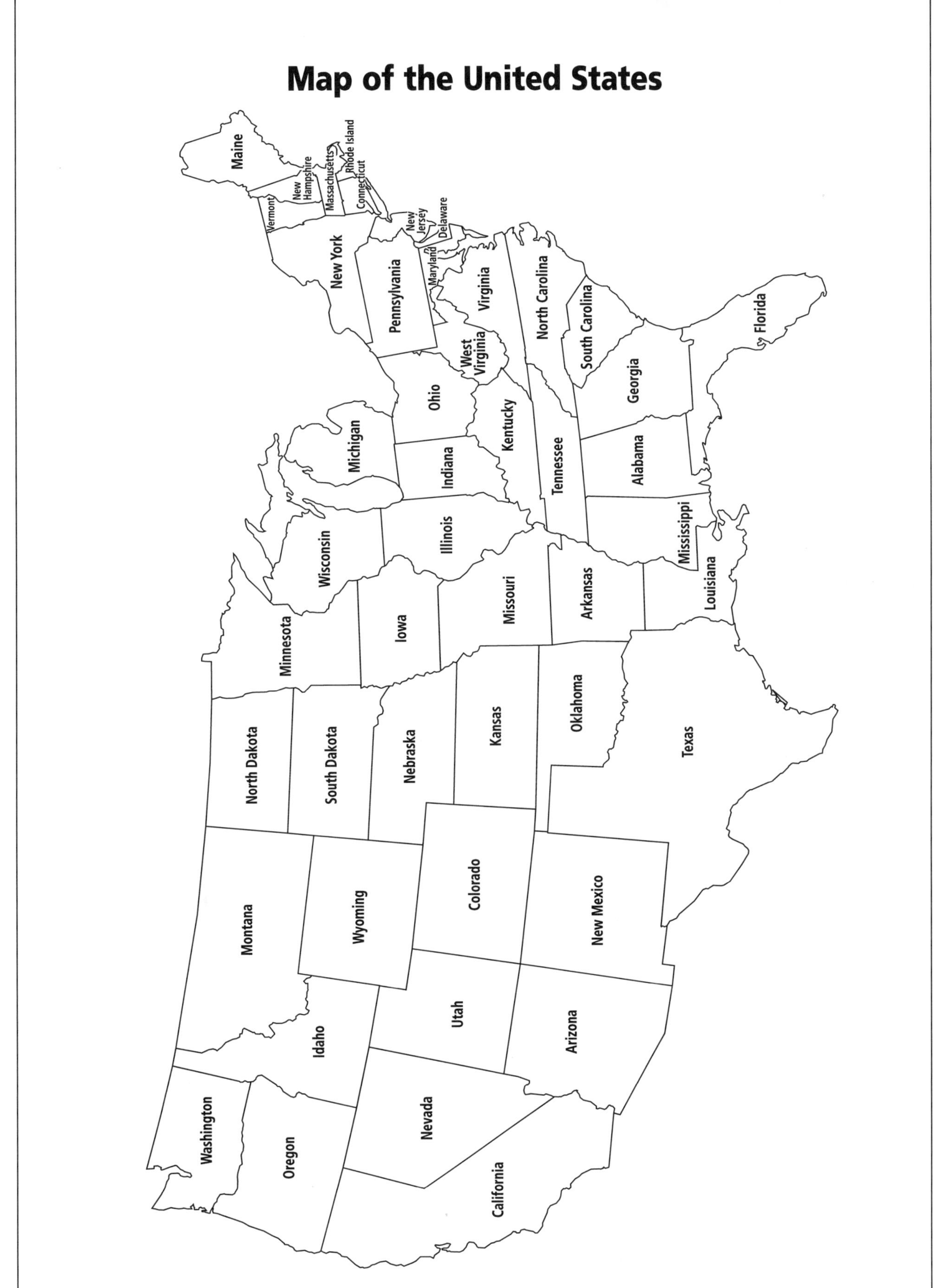

Base Ten Blocks

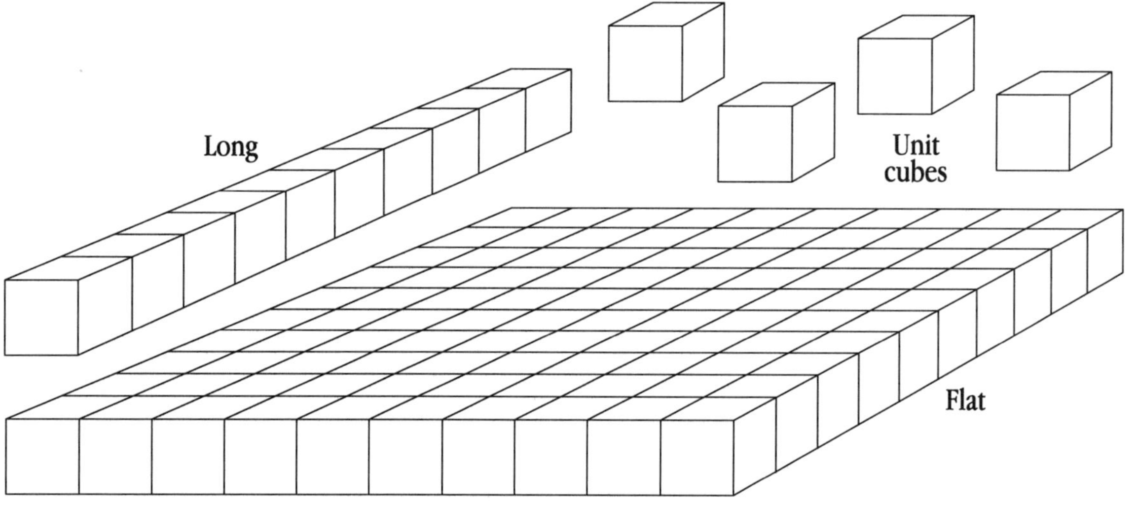

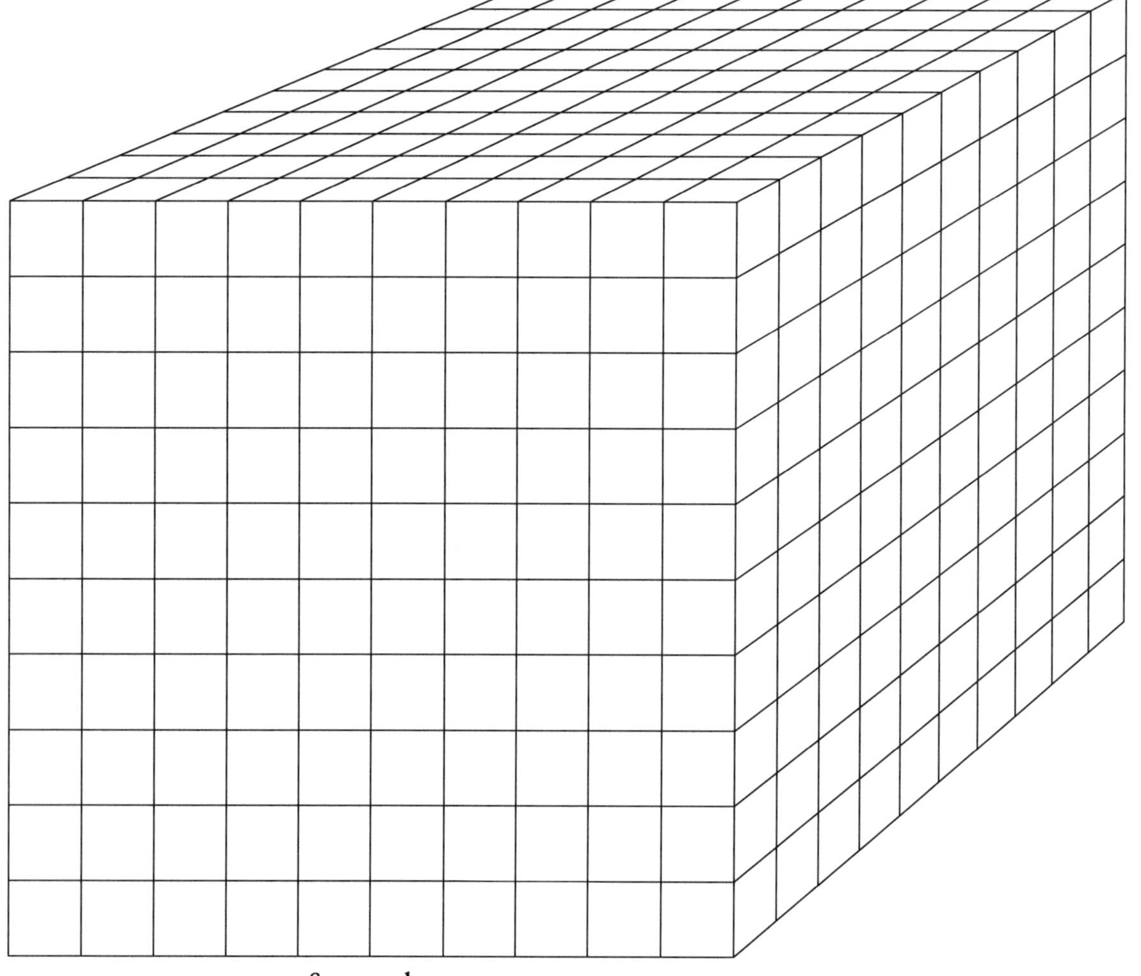

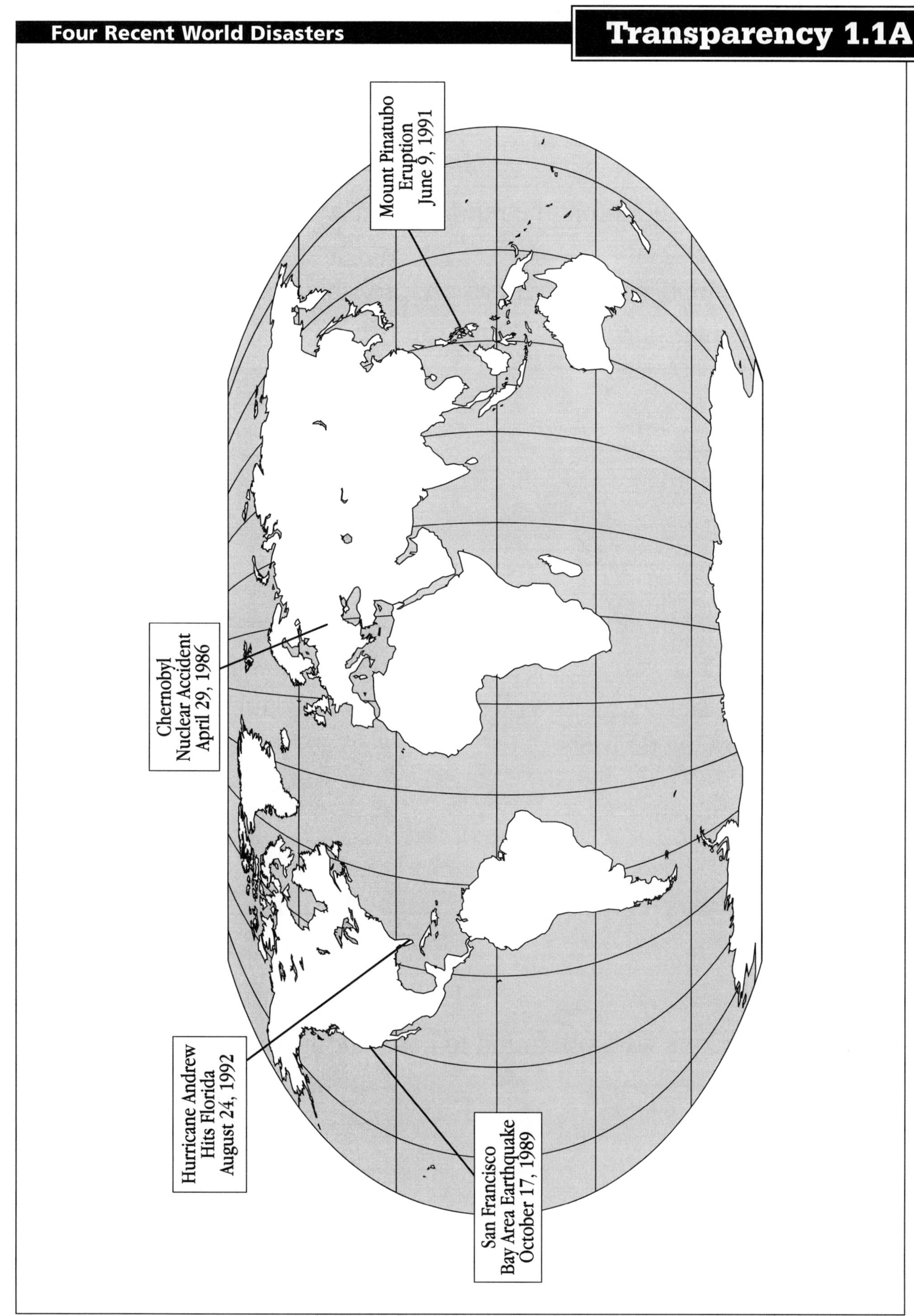
Mount Pinatubo
Eruption
June 9, 1991
Chernobyl
Nuclear Accident
April 29, 1986
Hurricane Andrew
Hits Florida
August 24, 1992
San Francisco
Bay Area Earthquake
October 17, 1989

Use the information from the reports to answer parts A–C.

A. Which numbers in the reports are probably very accurate, and which are probably only rough estimates?

B. Imagine that you are a journalist writing a story about these four disasters. Write several statements you could use to compare the disasters.

C. Describe the ways you found to compare the disasters.

The United States Marine Corps and the American Red Cross sent relief supplies for families left homeless by the hurricane.

A. The U.S. Marines offered tents. Suppose each tent held 18 sleeping cots and covered 500 square feet of ground. Tell what assumptions you make to answer each question.

1. How many tents would have been needed to take care of all the homeless?

2. How much ground area would have been needed for all these tents?

3. How does the area of one tent compare with the area of your classroom?

4. How many people do you think could sleep in your classroom if a disaster struck your town? How many people do you think could sleep in your school?

B. The Red Cross provided cots, blankets, food, and water for the tent city and other shelters. They set up 126 feeding stations and 230 shelters. Tell what assumptions you make to answer each question.

1. If each person received at least one meal a day, about how many meals did each feeding station have to provide each day?

2. About how many students are served in your school's cafeteria each day?

3. How many cafeterias like your school's would be needed to serve 250,000 people?

4. The shelters housed a total of 85,154 people. What was the average number of people per shelter?

Shortly after A __________ on B __________ a giant oil tanker left Valdez, Alaska, with a load of C __________ of crude oil from the Alaskan pipeline. To avoid icebergs, the ship took a course about D __________ out of the normal shipping channel. Unfortunately, less than E __________ later the ship ran aground on the underwater Bligh Reef. The rocks of the reef tore a F __________ gash in the tanker's hull, and G __________ of crude oil spilled onto the surface of Prince William Sound. For weeks, the world watched closely as the *Exxon Valdez* oil spill became an environmental disaster, despite extensive efforts to contain and clean up the oil. The spill gradually spread to form an oil slick, covering H __________ of water and killing I __________ sea otters and J __________ birds. The cleanup engaged K __________ of boats and workers, who struggled against the cold of L __________ water and air temperatures. The cleanup cost was over M __________, including N __________ for wildlife rescue alone.

Match each lettered blank with the correct measurement or range of numbers from the list below.

800 square miles	10,080,000 gallons	$41 million
2000 to 3000	600-foot	2 miles
40° Fahrenheit	150 centimeters	90,000 to 300,000
$2 billion	March 24, 1989	52,000,000 gallons
thousands	3 hours	9:00 P.M.

A. In your group, think of as many units of length, area, volume, weight or mass, temperature, and time as you can. Record each unit on a stick-on note. Be sure to think of both customary and metric units.

B. Group the units by the attributes they measure. Put all the units of length together, all the units of area together, and so on.

C. For each unit, try to think of something familiar that is about the size of 1 unit. For example, a sheet of notebook paper is about 1 foot long. A single-serving container of yogurt holds about 1 cup. Add each example to the stick-on note with the unit name. You can use these examples as benchmarks to help you imagine the size of something when a measurement is given.

Imagine you are a newspaper reporter assigned to the *Exxon Valdez* story. Use your own ideas or the hints given to write statements communicating each fact in a way that would be easy for your readers to understand.

A. *The* Exxon Valdez *spilled 10,080,000 gallons of crude oil.*
Hint: An Olympic-size swimming pool holds about 500,000 gallons of water. How many such pools could be filled with the 10,080,000 gallons of oil?

B. *The tanker strayed about 2 miles out of the usual shipping channel.*
Hint: What places in your area are about 2 miles apart?

C. *The water and air temperatures during the oil spill cleanup were about 40° Fahrenheit.*
Hint: When, if ever, do the water and air temperatures in your area reach these temperatures? Do you go swimming then?

D. *The tanker ran aground on Bligh Reef less than 3 hours after it left port.*
Hint: What familiar events last about 3 hours?

E. *The oil spill killed 90,000 to 300,000 seabirds.*
Hint: Consult an almanac or atlas to find cities or towns in your state with human populations about this size.

F. *The entire cleanup operation cost $2,000,000,000.*
Hint: In the United States, the mean annual pay for workers is about $25,000. How many annual salaries could be paid from the cleanup cost of the oil spill?

G. *The oil slick eventually covered 800 square miles of the water's surface.*
Hint: 1 mile is 5280 feet, so 1 square mile is $5280 \times 5280 =$ 27,878,400 square feet. Estimate the area of your classroom floor. Then, figure out how many such classroom floors it would take to cover 1 square mile and to cover the 800-square-mile oil slick.

Play Dialing Digits several times with different opponents. Record any strategies you find that help you win.

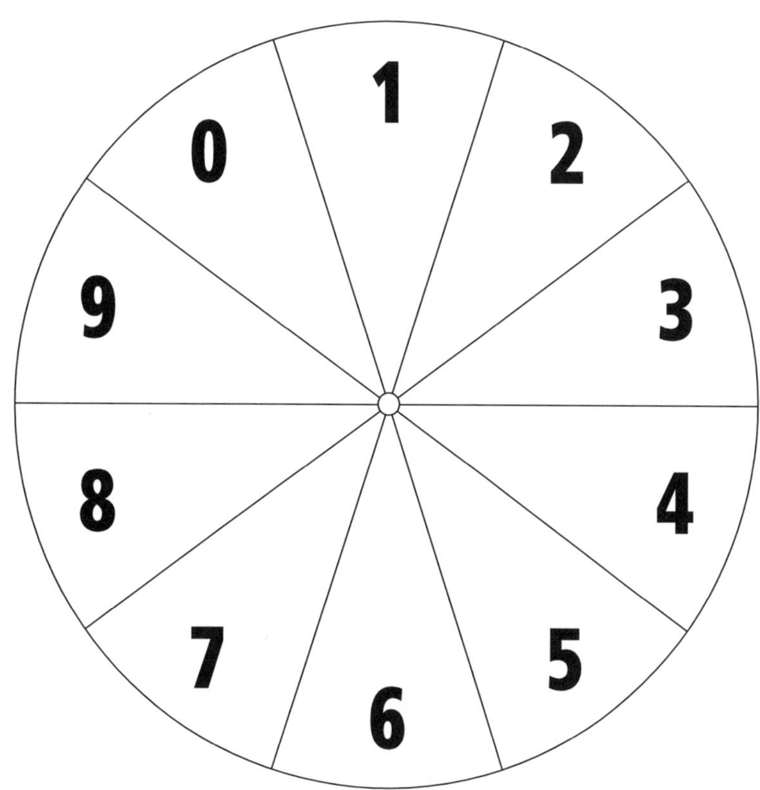

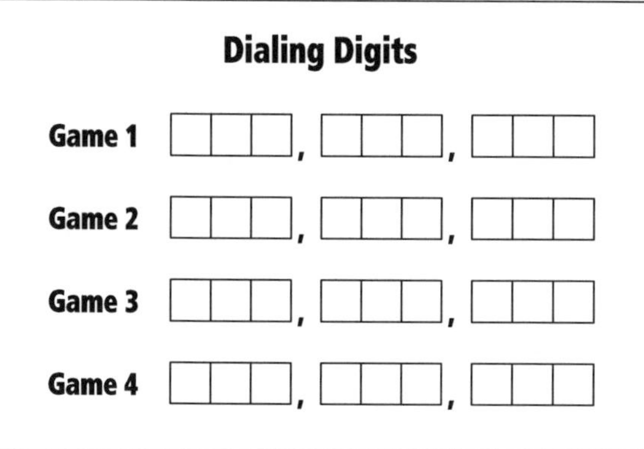

Dialing Digits

Game 1 ___ , ___ , ___

Game 2 ___ , ___ , ___

Game 3 ___ , ___ , ___

Game 4 ___ , ___ , ___

Metropolitan area	Population
Atlanta	2,959,950
Boston	5,455,403
Chicago	8,239,820
Cleveland	2,859,644
Dallas	4,037,282
Detroit	5,187,171
Houston	3,731,131
Los Angeles	14,531,529
Miami	3,192,582
Minneapolis	2,538,834
New York City	19,549,649
Philadelphia	5,892,937
Phoenix	2,238,480
Pittsburgh	2,394,811
St. Louis	2,492,525
San Diego	2,498,016
San Francisco	6,253,311
Seattle	2,970,328
Tampa	2,067,959
Washington, D.C.	6,727,050

The census data are given in alphabetical order, but it is often interesting and important to look at *ranking* by size.

A. Order the 20 metropolitan areas from most populated to least populated.

B. Describe some ways you could compare the populations of these metropolitan areas.

C. Locate each of the 20 metropolitan areas on the U.S. map on Labsheet 3.2. Look for interesting patterns in their locations.

1. What geographic factors seem to lead to large population centers?

2. How do you think the locations of these large metropolitan areas affect national and state government and business decisions?

Seattle
Minneapolis
Boston
Detroit
Chicago
Cleveland
Pittsburgh
New York City
Philadelphia
San Francisco
Washington, D.C.
St. Louis
Los Angeles
San Diego
Phoenix
Atlanta
Dallas
Houston
Tampa
Miami

In 1990, the population of the United States was reported to be 248,709,873. Here are four possible roundings of this number:

200,000,000 250,000,000 249,000,000 248,700,000

A. The population of the world is about 5.7 billion. Which of the above roundings would you use if you wanted to compare the population of the United States with the population of the world? Give reasons for your choice.

B. The population of India is about 1 billion. Which rounding would you use if you wanted to compare the population of the United States with the population of India? Give reasons for your choice.

C. In 1980, the population of the United States was about 226,000,000. Which rounding would you use if you wanted to compare the 1990 U.S. population with this 1980 population figure? Give reasons for your choice.

Transparency 3.4

County	1993 hog population	Growth from 1983	Hogs per square mile
Sampson	1,152,000	363%	1218
Duplin	1,041,000	349%	1273
Wayne	333,000	265%	603
Bladen	271,000	1178%	310
Greene	231,000	82%	870
Pitt	193,000	128%	297
Lenoir	159,000	312%	399
Johnston	129,000	61%	163
Robeson	124,000	81%	131
Onslow	115,000	261%	150
Jones	105,000	999%	223
Beaufort	103,000	51%	125
Pender	97,000	588%	111
Halifax	82,000	18%	113
Northampton	81,000	53%	151

Source: U.S. Department of Agriculture, as reported in the *Raleigh News and Observer,* 19–26 February 1995.

A. Write at least three statements comparing the hog data for Johnston County with the hog data for Bladen County.

B. Choose two different pairs of counties from the table. For each pair, write at least three statements comparing the hog data for the two counties.

For each part of this problem, explain your answer.

A. How long does it take your heart to beat 1,000,000 times?

B. Advertisements for a popular brand of chocolate chip cookie claim that there are 1000 chips in each bag of cookies. How many bags would you need to have 1,000,000 chips? If one bag measures 20 centimeters by 12 centimeters by 6 centimeters, would all of these bags fit in your classroom?

C. If someone is 1,000,000 hours old, what is his or her age in years?

D. How many students can stand inside a square with an area of 1,000,000 square centimeters?

A. How many unit cubes are needed to make one *flat*?

B. You can stack ten flats to make a *super cube.* How many unit cubes are needed to make a super cube?

C. You can line up ten super cubes to make a *super long.* How many unit cubes are needed to make a super long?

D. You can put together ten super longs to make a *super flat.* How many unit cubes are needed to make a super flat?

E. You can put together ten super flats to make a *super-duper cube.* How many unit cubes are needed to make a super-duper cube?

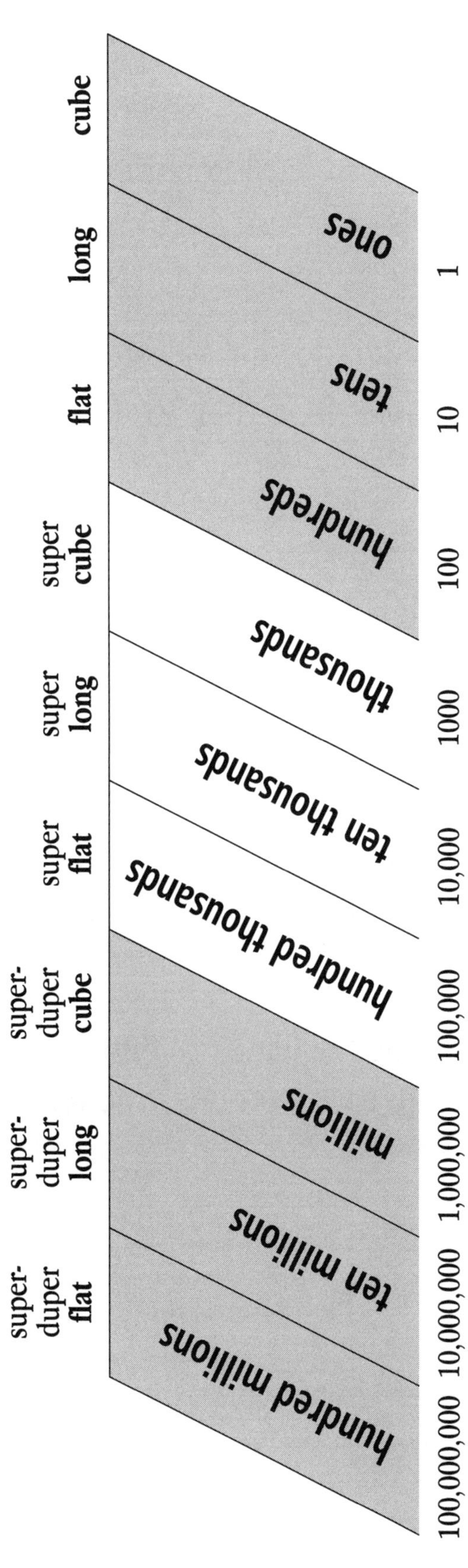
cube
long
flat
super cube
super long
super flat
super-duper cube
super-duper long
super-duper flat
ones
tens
hundreds
thousands
ten thousands
hundred thousands
millions
ten millions
hundred millions
1
10
100
1000
10,000
100,000
1,000,000
10,000,000
100,000,000

Transparency 4.3

Problem 4.3

A. Write each number in standard notation.

1. 10^{22} **2.** 10^{13} **3.** 10^{11} **4.** 10^{10}

B. Write each number in a shorter form by using an exponent.

1. $10 \times 10 \times 10 \times 10 \times 10 \times 10 \times 10 \times 10 \times 10 \times 10 \times 10 \times 10$

2. 1,000,000

C. Write each number in standard notation.

1. 3.0×10^9 **2.** 2.5×10^{13} **3.** 1.75×10^{10}

D. Write each number in scientific notation.

1. 5,000,000 **2.** 18,000,000 **3.** 17,900,000,000

E. Experiment with your calculator to find out how to get these displays. Then, write each number in scientific and standard notation.

1. `1.7E12` or `1.7    12`

2. `1.7E15` or `1.7    15`

3. `2.35E12` or `2.35    12`

4. `3.698E16` or `3.698    16`

Transparency 5.1

County	1993 hog population	Growth from 1983	Hogs per square mile
Sampson	1,152,000	363%	1218
Duplin	1,041,000	349%	1273
Wayne	333,000	265%	603
Bladen	271,000	1178%	310
Greene	231,000	82%	870

Source: U.S. Department of Agriculture, as reported in the *Raleigh News and Observer,* 19–26 February 1995.

Assume the growth of the hog populations continues at the rates given in the table for the ten years from 1993 to 2003.

A. Predict the number of hogs in each county at the end of the year 2003. Which counties will have over a million hogs?

B. Will the ranking of these five counties be the same in 2003 as it was in 1993? Explain your answer.

Transparency 5.2

A. Take a class survey, asking each student to estimate the number of soft drink cans he or she uses in a typical week. Make a line plot of the data, and find the mean and the median.

B. Estimate the number of cans used by all the students in your class in one day, one week, one month, and one year.

C. Estimate the number of cans used by all the students in your school in one day, one week, one month, and one year.

D. Estimate the number of cans used by all 260,000,000 Americans in one day, one week, one month, and one year.

Transparency 5.3

A. Time yourself as you brush your teeth, and record the total brushing time. Then, let the water run from the faucet into a large pan for 10 seconds. Use a measuring cup to find the amount of water collected. Use these data to figure out how much water you would use if you let the water run while you brushed your teeth.

B. Collect the data for the entire class on the board. Then, find the average amount of water used per student.

C. Suppose everyone let the water run while brushing their teeth. Estimate the amount of water that would be used by your class for toothbrushing in a typical year. Assume each student brushes twice a day. Extend your estimate to find the amount of water that would be used yearly by all 260,000,000 Americans just for toothbrushing.

Suppose municipal waste could be compacted into cubes measuring 1 foot on each edge. Each such cube would be composed of about 50 pounds of waste.

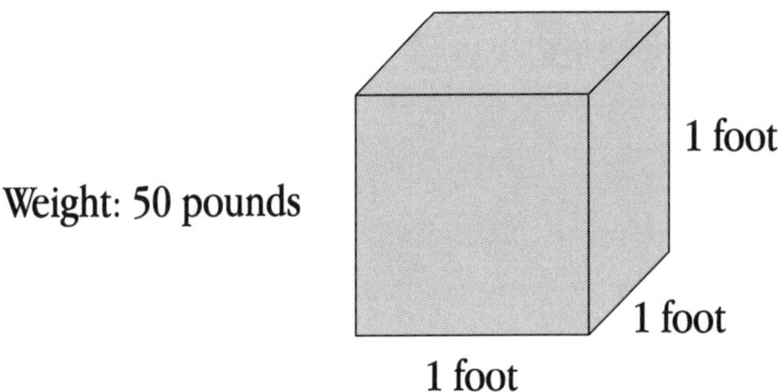

If all the municipal waste collected from American homes, businesses, and industries were pressed into 1-foot waste cubes, how many cubes would be produced in just one day?

On an average day in Japan, about 52,055,000 aluminum cans are used. Japan's population of 123 million people recycles 34,356,000 of those cans. In the United States, which has a population of 250 million people, about 93,310,000 aluminum cans are used on an average day, and about half of them are recycled.

A. How many aluminum cans are *not* recycled in Japan on an average day?

B. How many aluminum cans are *not* recycled in the United States on an average day?

C. In an average week, how many aluminum cans are used in each country? How many cans are recycled?

For each statement, compare the data about life in Japan and the United States in the two ways described in your math book, and decide which comparison better explains the similarities or differences.

A. The average Japanese child spends 275 hours each year playing sports and games. The average American child spends 550 hours each year in these activities.

B. The average American has $10,000 in savings accounts. The average Japanese has $40,000 saved.

C. On an average day, Japanese children spend 7 hours in school, and American children spend 5 hours 25 minutes in school.

D. The average American makes 200 telephone calls each month. The average Japanese makes 45 calls each month.

E. On an average day, 40% of Japanese use public transportation, while fewer than 4% of Americans do.

Transparency 6.3

The table gives data about smoking in the United States and Japan.

Country	Population	Smokers	Total cigarettes smoked each day
United States	250,000,000	55,000,000	1,437,315,000
Japan	123,000,000	33,000,000	849,315,000

A. Compare the number of smokers in the two countries in as many ways as you can. Which comparison do you believe is best?

B. Compare the number of cigarettes smoked each day in the two countries in as many ways as you can. Which comparison do you believe is best?

Family Letter (English)

Dear Family,

The last unit in your child's course of study in mathematics class this year is *Data Around Us.* In this unit, students will study large numbers as they occur in such contexts as accounts of natural disasters like hurricanes, earthquakes, volcanoes, and floods. Very large numbers are reported in the news every day, yet many people have a difficult time grasping their meaning.

As they look at the populations of large cities, the U.S. national debt, or the numbers of smokers in different countries, students will order and compare large numbers and get familiar with certain benchmarks that will help them to form ideas about the magnitudes of the numbers with which they are dealing.

You might help your child by observing the use of large numbers in the newspaper, and talking about them with your child. Here are some other strategies for helping your child work with the ideas in this unit:

- Ask your child to describe some of the real-world situations in which very large or very small numbers are used. Listen with your child to the ways very large and very small numbers are presented in news reports.
- Look at your child's mathematics notebook. You may want to review some of the explanations your child has written for new concepts and talk with your child about them if they aren't clear.
- Encourage your child's efforts in completing all homework assignments.

As always, if you have any questions or concerns about this unit or your child's progress in the class, please feel free to call. We are always interested in your child's success in mathematics.

Sincerely,

Estimada familia,

La última unidad del programa de matem·ticas de su hijo o hija para este curso se llama *Data Around Us* (Datos de nuestro entorno). En ella los alumnos estudiar·n grandes cifras que aparecen en contextos como, por ejemplo, los informes sobre los desastres naturales: huracanes, terremotos, volcanes e inundaciones. Todos los días encóntramos cifras enormes en las noticias y, sin embargo, a muchas personas les cuesta imaginar su magnitud.

Los alumnos, al examinar la población de grandes ciudades, la deuda nacional de los EE.UU. o el número de fumadores que hay en distintos países, ordenarán y compararán grandes cifras y se familiarizarán con ciertas referencias, las cuales les ayudarán a formar ideas sobre las magnitudes de dichos números.

Será de ayuda a su hijo o hija que ustedes le muestren cómo se emplean las grandes cifras en el periódico y que luego las comenten juntos. Aparecen a continuación algunas estrategias adicionales que ustedes pueden emplear para ayudar a su hijo o hija con las ideas de esta unidad:

- Pídanle que describa algunas de las situaciones del mundo real en las que se utilicen cifras muy grandes o muy pequeñas. Escuchen juntos el noticiero para ver en quÈ formas se presentan dichos n˙meros.
- Miren su cuaderno de matemáticas. Es recomendable que repasen algunas de las explicaciones que su hijo o hija ha escrito sobre los nuevos conceptos y que comenten juntos las que no resulten claras.
- Anímenle a esforzarse para que complete toda la tarea.

Y como de costumbre, si ustedes necesitan m·s detalles o aclaraciones respecto a la unidad o sobre los progresos de su hijo o hija en esta clase, no duden en llamarnos. Nos interesa en todo momento que su hijo o hija avance en el estudio de las matemáticas.

Atentamente,

Additional Practice

Investigation 1

Use these problems for additional practice after Investigation 1.

1. During the Revolutionary War, 250,000 people served in the U.S. armed forces and there were 33,769 casualties. In World War II, 16,353,659 people served in the U.S. armed forces and there were 1,078,162 casualties.*

   a. Which do you think is more accurate, the data for the Revolutionary War or the data for World War II? Explain your reasoning.

   b. What percent of those who served during the Revolutionary War were casualties?

   c. What percent of those who served during World War II were casualties?

   d. Was a person serving in the U.S. armed forces during the Revolutionary War more or less likely to become a casualty compared with a person serving during World War II? Explain your reasoning.

2. In 1987, the population of the United States was 245 million. In that year, 2,279,000 people served in the U.S. armed forces.

   a. Do you think the data for the 1987 U.S. population and for the total number of U.S. armed forces personnel are exact numbers or estimates? Explain your reasoning.

   b. What percent of the U.S. population served in the armed forces in 1987?

   c. In 1987 the United States was not at war. During times of war, the percent of people serving in the armed forces may increase considerably. How many people would have served in the U.S. armed forces in 1987 if the percent were 8 times greater than the percent you found in part b?

*Source: *The World Almanac and Book of Facts 1996.* Ed. Robert Famighetti. Mahwa, New Jersey: Funk and Wagnalls, 1995.

Investigation 2

Use these problems for additional practice after Investigation 2.

1. During the 1991–92 school year, 1141 students were enrolled at Metropolis Middle School.

   a. If student enrollment increased by 8.1% the following year, how many students were enrolled at Metropolis Middle School during the 1992–93 year?

   b. During the 1993–94 school year, there were 1253 students at Metropolis Middle School, and during the 1995–96 school year, enrollment was 1354. What was the percent increase in enrollment over the two years?

   c. Do you think the enrollment data for Metropolis Middle School are exact figures or estimates? Explain your reasoning.

2. The number of teachers at Metropolis Middle School during the 1991–92 school year was 51 (with 1141 students), and the number of teachers during the 1995–96 school year was 55 (with 1354 students).

   a. What was the ratio of students to teachers at Metropolis Middle School for the 1991–92 year? Explain how you found your answer.

   b. What was the ratio of students to teachers at Metropolis Middle School for the 1995–96 year?

   c. What was the percent change (that is, the percent increase or decrease) in the ratio of students to teachers from 1991–92 to 1995–96? Explain how you found your answer.

   d. Based on your answer to part c, would you say that the increase in the number of teachers at Metropolis Middle School has kept up with the increase in student enrollment? Explain your reasoning.

3. A typical midsize car has a curb weight (that is, a weight without passengers) of about 3000 pounds. A typical bowling ball weighs about 12 pounds.

   a. How many 12-pound bowling balls would it take to equal the weight of a midsize car? Explain how you found your answer.

   b. A typical full-size family truck weighs about 4200 pounds. How many 12-pound bowling balls would it take to equal the weight of a full-size truck?

Investigation 3

Use these problems for additional practice after Investigation 3.

1. For the 1995–96 school year, the total budget of Omega College was $28,325,800, and student enrollment was 1437.
   a. In the 1995–96 school year, tuition and fees paid by students made up 68.3% of the school's budget. What was the total cost for tuition and fees per student at Omega College? Explain how you found your answer.
   b. For the 1996–97 school year, the budget of Omega College increased by 4.2%, and tuition and fees for each student increased by $405. Which increased by the greatest percent—the college budget or tuition and fees? Explain your reasoning.
   c. In 1995–96, 26.1% of the college budget went toward faculty salaries. Estimate the amount for faculty salaries to the nearest million dollars. Explain your estimation strategy.
2. The Omega College library contains 390,000 books. There are 1437 students enrolled at the school.
   a. Estimate the number of books in the Omega College library per student to the nearest ten, and explain your estimation strategy.
   b. Estimate the number of books Omega College would have to add to the library to raise the number of books per student to 300. Explain your estimation strategy.
   c. What would the percent change in the number of books per student need to be to increase the current number of books per student to 300? Explain how you estimated the percent.
3. A lottery game advertises a jackpot of $41 million. The chances of a ticket having the winning numbers are 1 in 7.1 million.
   a. If Betty buys 10 lottery tickets, what are her chances of winning? Explain your reasoning.
   b. How many lottery tickets would Betty have to buy if she wanted to increase her chances of winning to 1 in 71?

Investigation 4

Use these problems for additional practice after Investigation 4.

1. In astronomy, a *light year* is 5,880,000,000,000 miles.
   a. Write the number of miles in one light year in scientific notation.
   b. Write the number of miles in 100 light years in scientific notation. Explain your reasoning.
   c. The distance between two stars is 3×10^{11} miles. Without using your calculator, estimate how many light years apart the stars are. Explain how you found your answer.

2. Another unit used in astronomy to measure large distances is the *parsec*, which is equal to 3.26 light years.
   a. How many miles are there in a parsec? Explain your reasoning.
   b. Two planets are 2.7×10^{14} miles apart. What is the distance between the planets in parsecs?
   c. The *speed of light* is 186,000 miles per second. Moving at the speed of light, how many seconds would it take to travel a parsec?
   d. Would it make more sense to express the time it takes to travel a parsec when moving at light speed in a unit other than seconds? Explain your reasoning.

3. Sylvia can walk briskly at a rate of about 4 miles per hour.
   a. How long would it take Sylvia to walk 10 miles?
   b. Based on your answer to part a, how long would it take Sylvia to walk 100 miles? Explain your reasoning.
   c. Do you think it might actually take Sylvia longer to walk 100 miles than your answer in part b? Explain your reasoning.
   d. If Sylvia walks at 4 miles per hour for three hours each week, how long will it take her to cover 1000 miles?
   e. Do you think that Sylvia will be able to cover 100,000 miles in her lifetime? Explain your reasoning.

Investigation 5

Use these problems for additional practice after Investigation 5.

1. Francesca bought a plot of land measuring 1 square mile on which she plans to grow grapes. She hires 346 people to plant seedlings. It takes about 20 seconds to plant each seedling, and each seedling requires 1.5 square feet of area.
   a. How many square feet of land can the 346 workers plant each minute?
   b. How much time will it take to plant the entire plot of land? Explain your reasoning.
   c. Francesca decides to plant a different type of grape that requires only 1.2 square feet of land per seedling. How much time will it take the workers to plant these seedlings?

2. Trevor's mother commutes to work. Her round-trip drive from home to work and back is 78 miles. She works Monday through Friday.
   a. How many miles per week does Trevor's mother drive in commuting to work?
   b. If Trevor's mother works 49 weeks per year, how many miles does she drive in commuting to work each year?
   c. Based on your answer to part b, if Trevor's mother's car gets 34 miles per gallon, how many gallons of gas does she use each year commuting to and from work?

3. Americans use about 50 million tons of paper made from 850 million trees each year.*
   a. How many trees does it take to produce one ton of paper?
   b. What is the weight of the paper produced by one tree?
   c. Suppose that through recycling we could reduce the amount of paper consumed by 16.5%. How many trees would that save each year? Explain your reasoning.

*Source: Rebecca Stefoff. *Recycling*. New York: Chelsea House, 1991.

Investigation 6

Use these problems for additional practice after Investigation 6.

1. There are 1358 students and 68 teachers at Metropolis Middle School. On a typical day, students spend a total of $1562 on lunches and teachers spend a total of $135.
   a. How much does the average student spend per day on lunch?
   b. How much does the average teacher spend per day on lunch?
   c. Express as a percent how much more money is spent on lunches by the average teacher than by the average student.
2. Last year at Metropolis Middle School, 27 girls and 34 boys tried out for basketball.
   a. If the number of girls who tried out for basketball this year is 25% higher than the number who tried out last year, about how many girls tried out for basketball this year?
   b. This year, 31 boys tried out for basketball. What is the percent change in the number of boys who tried out this year compared to last year?
   c. There are 1358 students at Metropolis Middle School. Based on parts a and b above, what percent of all students tried out for basketball this year?
3. Carlos buys a candy bar twice each week. Each candy bar costs $0.55.
   a. How many candy bars does Carlos buy each year?
   b. How much money does Carlos spend on candy bars each year?
   c. One of the clerks at the store told Carlos that, starting next year, the price of the candy bars will increase by 15%.
      i. What will the new price of the candy bars be?
      ii. If Carlos continues to buy two candy bars per week, how much more money will he spend on candy bars over the next year than he did over the past year?

Investigation 1

1. a. The World War II data are probably more accurate due to better communication and record-keeping.
   b. 13.5%
   c. 6.6%
   d. A person serving in the armed forces during the Revolutionary War was about twice as likely to become a casualty since $13.5 \div 6.6$ is about 2.

2. a. The data are probably estimates because they are round numbers and because finding exact counts would be difficult or impossible.
   b. 0.93%
   c. 18,232,000

Investigation 2

1. a. 1233
   b. 8.06%
   c. The data are probably exact, since the population is fairly small and schools tend to keep careful records.

2. a. 22.4 to 1; The ratio is $\frac{1141}{51}$, or about $\frac{22.4}{1}$.
   b. 24.6 to 1
   c. The ratio increased by 2.2 students, an increase of $\frac{2.2}{22.4} = 9.8\%$.
   d. no; The ratio of students to teachers has increased. This means that the increase in the number of teachers has not kept pace with the increase in student enrollment.

3. a. $3000 \div 12 = 250$ bowling balls
   b. $4200 \div 12 = 350$ bowling balls

Investigation 3

1. a. Tuition and fees were $0.0683 \times \$28,325,800 = \$19,346,521$. Per student, this is $\$19,346,521 \div 1437 = \$13,463$.
   b. Tuition and fees increased by $\frac{405}{13,463}$, or 3%, so the budget increase was more.
   c. 26.1% is about 25%, which is $\frac{1}{4}$, and $\frac{1}{4}$ of the \$28,325,800 budget is about $\frac{1}{4}$ of \$28,000,000, which is \$7,000,000.

2. a. $\frac{390,000}{1437}$ is about $\frac{400}{1.5}$, which is about 270 books per student.
   b. They would need 30 more books per student. Rounding the number of students to 1400, they need about $30 \times 1400 = 42,000$ more books in the library.
   c. about 11.1%

3. a. Her chances are now 10 in 71,000,000, or 1 in 710,000.
   b. Betty would have to buy 100,000 tickets.

Investigation 4

1. a. 5.88×10^{12} miles
   b. 5.88×10^{14} miles; Multiplying by 100 adds two more 0s.
   c. Round a light year to 6×10^{12} miles, then $\frac{3 \times 10^{11}}{6 \times 10^{12}} = \frac{3}{6 \times 10^{1}} = \frac{3}{60} = \frac{1}{20}$ light year.

2. a. $3.26 \times (5.88 \times 10^{12}) = 1.917 \times 10^{13}$ miles in a parsec
   b. $(2.7 \times 10^{14}) \div (1.917 \times 10^{13}) = 14.1$ parsecs apart.
   c. $(1.917 \times 10^{13}) \div 186{,}000 = 1.03 \times 10^{8}$ seconds
   d. Yes, since it is hard to imagine such a large number of seconds, expressing the answer in years would help us make sense of the answer. It would take 3.27 years, traveling at the speed of light, to travel 1 parsec. (There are $365 \times 24 \times 60 \times 60 = 3.1536 \times 10^{7}$ seconds in 1 year.)

3. a. 2.5 hours
   b. 10×2.5 hours $= 25$ hours
   c. yes; She needs to rest!
   d. Sylvia would walk $4 \times 3 = 12$ miles per week and $12 \times 52 = 624$ miles per year, so it would take her $1000 \div 624 = 1.6$ years to walk 1000 miles.
   e. no; Walking 4 miles per hour, 3 hours per week, it would take Sylvia 160 years to walk 100,000 miles!

Investigation 5

1. a. 1557 square feet
   b. There are $(5280 \text{ feet})^2 = 27{,}878{,}400$ square feet available. It will take $\frac{27{,}878{,}400}{1557} \approx 17{,}905$ minutes, or about 298 hours to plant the entire plot.
   c. about 373 hours

2. a. 390 miles
   b. 19,110 miles
   c. 562 gallons per year

3. **a.** about 17 trees
   b. 117.6 pounds
   c. 850,000,000 trees × 0.165 = 140,250,000 trees

Investigation 6

1. **a.** $1.15
   b. $1.99
   c. Teachers spend 73% more on their lunches than do students.

2. **a.** 34
   b. ⁻8.8%
   c. 4.8%

3. **a.** 104
   b. $57.20
   c. **i.** $0.63
   ii. Will spend $8.58 more for the year.

Descriptive Glossary

benchmark A handy reference point to help in understanding the magnitude of other numbers. When working with decimals or fractions, we sometimes use whole numbers and halves as benchmarks, rounding the decimals or fractions to the nearest half. Benchmarks can help us to make sense of the magnitude of a very large number. If the *Exxon Valdez* disaster cost $20,000,000,000 to clean up and the average annual pay for a U.S. worker is $25,000, looking at the number of annual salaries required to pay the cleanup bill can help us to understand the magnitude of this cost. In this example, $25,000 is used as a benchmark.

customary system A complex measurement system that originated primarily in the British empire and includes the units of measure inch, yard, pound, and gallon. The system was in use in the United States from the nation's beginnings and is still used today in many situations. In commercial and scientific applications, the metric system is becoming more and more common.

metric system, international system of measurement, SI system A measurement system used throughout the world that is based on the power of 10. The basic units of length, volume, and mass are the meter, liter, and gram, respectively.

million, billion, trillion The numbers 1,000,000 (or 10^6), 1,000,000,000 (or 10^9), and 1,000,000,000,000 (or 10^{12}), respectively.

scientific notation A short way to write very large or very small numbers. A number written in scientific notation is expressed in this form:

a number greater than or equal to 1 but less than 10	×	10 raised to an exponent

standard notation The most common form of written numbers. For example, 254 is the standard notation for 2 hundreds, 5 tens, and 4 ones.

medida de referencia Un punto de referencia de utilidad para comprender la magnitud de otros números. A veces, al trabajar con números decimales o fracciones, utilizamos números enteros y mitades como medidas de referencia, redondeando dichos números decimales o fracciones a la mitad más cercana. Las medidas de referencia pueden ayudarnos a comprender la magnitud de un número muy grande. Por ejemplo, si limpiar la zona afectada por el desastre del *Exxon Valdez* costó 20,000,000,000 y el sueldo anual medio de un trabajador de EE.UU. es de $25,000, podemos calcular el número de sueldos anuales necesarios para pagar los gastos de la limpieza y así ayudarnos a comprender la magnitud del costo. En este ejemplo, $25,000 sirve como medida de referencia.

millón, mil millones, billón Los números 1,000,000 (ó 10^6), 1,000,000,000 (ó 10^9) y 1,000,000,000,000 (ó 10^{12}), respectivamente.

notación científica Una forma abreviada de escribir números muy grandes o muy pequeños. Un número escrito en notación científica se expresa de la siguiente manera: un número mayor que o igual a 1 pero menor que 10 $\times$ 10 elevado a un exponente

notación normal La forma más común de escribir números. Por ejemplo, 2 centenas, 5 decenas y 4 unidades se escribe en notación normal como 254.

sistema estadounidense Un complejo sistema de medición que tuvo su origen principalmente en el imperio británico y que incluye como unidades de medida la pulgada, la yarda, la libra y el galón. Este sistema se empleó en Estados Unidos desde sus inicios como nación y se sigue utilizando actualmente en una diversidad de situaciones. Por otra parte, en aplicaciones comerciales y científicas el uso del sistema métrico es cada vez más frecuente.

sistema métrico, sistema internacional de medidas, sistema SI Un sistema de medición utilizado en todo el mundo y que se basa en las potencias de 10. Las unidades fundamentales de longitud, volumen y masa son el metro, el litro y el gramo, respectivamente.

Index

Index

Index